¡Hablamos!

¡HABLAMOS!

Puerto Ricans Speak

Henrietta Yurchenco

PHOTOGRAPHS BY JULIA SINGER

PRAEGER PUBLISHERS
New York • Washington • London

PRAEGER PUBLISHERS
111 Fourth Avenue, New York, N.Y. 10003, U.S.A.
5, Cromwell Place, London, SW7 2JL, England

Published in the United States of America in 1971
by Praeger Publishers, Inc.

Library of Congress Catalog Card Number: 73–121721

Printed in the United States of America

To

S. Parilla de Falú

and

Antonio Martorell

Contents

Preface

My love for the Spanish-speaking world began more than thirty years ago in Mexico, and it developed later in Guatemala, Spain, and North Africa. I learned the language and lived in small towns, remote Indian villages, and large cities. I became comfortable with the ways of thinking and doing, the customs and traditions.

In a sense, then, I was not a stranger when I arrived in Puerto Rico in 1967 for the first time. I traveled around the Island on that first trip, looking, observing, and feeling. Mountains, clear blue-green waters and sandy beaches, flamboyant flowering trees, feathery sugar-cane blossoms swaying in the breeze—all cast a spell over me.

Time and again I returned. I sat on many porches, swapped recipes with the women, played games with the children, and listened to talk about everything from birth to death. In quiet mountain and coastal villages, the people talked about their private lives; their love for their country, the traditions they live by, and the changes that have come with industrialization. In the city, where social ferment bubbles, conversation was hot with opinions on social and political issues.

When I returned to New York, I had thirty-five hours of recorded interviews. Julia Singer, who had worked closely with me, had taken thousands of photographs. From my tapes, I selected the portions that would be most likely to help the reader understand the Puerto Ricans on the Island and therefore also the Puerto Ricans in their own communities in the States.

The stories, opinions, and beliefs of the people with whom I spoke are published here exactly as given to me (in English or in my translation from the Spanish, edited only for length).

I will ever be grateful to the people of the Island for opening their hearts to me, for helping me to accomplish my mission.

New York, New York
June, 1971

Acknowledgments

I wish to acknowledge my gratitude to the many people who made this book possible: To my friends Hally Wood Stephenson and Peter and Ellen Hawes for their hospitality and guidance; to Emilio Rodríguez Vásquez for transcriptions and translations; to Mika Seeger for her help in the research; to Marion Gutmann for preparing the final manuscript; to my husband, Irving Levine, for editing and for invaluable advice at every stage of the work; and my special thanks to the American Philosophical Society for a grant to aid me in this work.

H.Y.

List of Characters

(in order of appearance)

Doña Lola—an octogenarian who still remembers her childhood.

Minnie Roses—daughter of the owner of Hacienda Roses, once a flourishing coffee plantation.

Norberto Cedeño—a sculptor of popular artifacts, one of the last *santeros* (*santo* makers).

Castor Ayala—in his sixties, he is Loíza Aldea's most famous mask-maker and master craftsman, herb doctor and teller of tales.

Maí Vargas—an outspoken black Puerto Rican in her sixties who has lived all of her life in Loíza Aldea.

Sofía Vargas—Maí Vargas' eldest daughter, in her mid-thirties, spiritualist, widow, and mother of six. Independent and proud, she lives life according to her own principles, despite the disapproval of her neighbors.

Raúl Ayala—Castor Ayala's son, student at the University of Puerto Rico, and a fine drummer who loves the old traditions.

Mita (Juanita García Peraza)—the leader of a cult until her death in 1970. Her followers believe her to be the Prophet of the twentieth century.

Antonio Martorell—painter, graphic artist, and director of the Taller Alacrán.

Carmelo Martínez—subdirector of the Taller Alacrán.

Jorge David Echevarría ("Rolington"—named after the Rolling Stones)—a high school dropout and a dedicated student at the Taller Alacrán.

Fred Nasario—former Secretary of Labor under Muñoz Marín.

Milton Pabón—head of the Political Science Department of the University of Puerto Rico.

Nilita Vientos Gastón—literary critic, former Attorney General, and a leading intellectual figure of the Island.

Father Salvador Freixedo—a dissident Catholic priest who caused a furor with the publication of his book *Mi Iglesia Duerme* (*My Church Sleeps*).

¡Hablamos!

"We didn't have bad conditions . . . we didn't know what bad conditions were."

1

Doña Lola

Doña Lola, a vigorous lady of more than eighty years, has lived all her life in Certenejas, a mountain village near Cidra. Going down the road toward town, she looks like a ship in full sail. When a stranger asked, *"¿Usted es doña Dolores Velez de Colón?"* she boomed in a deep bass voice, with the air of a queen, *"Servidora"* [Your servant].

Peter Hawes, an American who has lived and worked near Cidra for many years, introduced me to Doña Lola, whose colorful story so clearly conveys the humor and joy of life—no matter how difficult life may be—that we found wherever we went in Puerto Rico.

Doña Lola: "In my youth, everybody around here lived happy, O.K. We didn't have bad conditions, because we didn't know what bad conditions were. My pop wasn't really rich, but he did all right. There was a school here, but none of us older kids went. The teacher would come to round us up, and you know what we'd do? Crawl under the table. We were that afraid of people! Me—what I liked to do was follow my papa around. He was quite a man! To go to school and not be with him? No sir! I didn't go and neither did the others. We'd help Papa harvest coffee, and also beans and corn, and dry rice. He had a couple of acres of rice. Nowadays you don't see a single twig of rice.

"Before I was married, I had a lot of fun. When Don Agustín Vil came from Río Piedras, he bought an enormous farm and planted tobacco. He brought peons to teach us how to work the tobacco, because it was the first time it was planted here. He hired girls to do some of the work. We built a barn to hang the tobacco

"Money was very scarce. . . . But we got 30 cents a day."

to dry, and then we sewed and put it together in bundles. His wife said to us, 'Well, girls, when we sell the crop, we'll have a party and dance to my piano.' We didn't know what a piano was and were crazy to see it. I, more than anyone.

"At dawn we went to the fields. At six o'clock we'd begin working. We'd plant five acres, and then five more. The peons earned 18 cents a day. Money was very scarce in those days. But we got 30 cents a day—35 cents if we worked until midnight.

"Finally the harvest was sold, and his wife sent each of us an invitation to a dance in their beautiful house. That lady was already pregnant. She sat on the string hammock and gave us sweets we never tasted before. She made rice pudding that was wet and juicy, the best I ever tasted. And every time she jumped up from the hammock, she gave us these fine drinks they call 'cock's tail' [in Spanish, *rabogallo*], and they didn't put us asleep!

"I was engaged to a boy for four and a half years. One night Papa told me, 'Lola, *caramba,* it's not because you're my daughter, but you deserve someone better than him.' There wasn't a sign he was ever going to earn a living or make a home for me. So I said to myself, how am I going to get rid of him? Papa's right. We wash and iron his clothes; we give him breakfast, lunch, dinner, and coffee. But one day his guilt got the better of him, and he bought me a pack of cigars [there were no cigarettes then], matches, and some candy, and left them in the house of my *compaí* [godmother].

"I was on my way to sing rosaries that night but left earlier so I could talk with my sister-in-law about my faults. I was kind of proud and conceited. God and the Virgin Mary forgive me! 'Here I am,' I said, 'tell me my faults. Better you tell me than some stranger in the street.'

"Then Guiso, her husband, handed me the package and said, 'Gabino' (that's my boyfriend's name) 'left this for you.' 'How nice,' I said, 'a present!' But I didn't touch it. 'Aren't you taking it?' asked my sister-in-law. 'No,' I said, 'it's been four and half years of friendship, and now it's over.' And I left to say my rosaries.

"When I saw Gabino, I said, 'Since you've been courting me, I've never done anything behind my mother and father's back, not even a puff of a cigar. Today it would be a puff, tomorrow this and that, and so on. But not with me!'

"And he said, 'You're angry with me for buying you cigars?' 'Oh no,' I said, 'you don't know how glad I am, because now everything's ended!'

"We spent that whole night praying and singing rosaries. I love to sing them. Every now and then, I'd come out for air, and that boy was always there. Things went on like before for a few days. Then he came to me and said, 'Lola, you're so serious these last few days.'

" 'Serious?' I said, 'Serious I'm going to *be,* sonny. You can have your breakfast, lunch, dinner, and coffee here and your clothes washed and ironed. When you get sick, we will take care of you, but our friendship is over. I have only two words, yes and no. And now everything is said.'

"He was a nice guy. His only fault was that he was lazy and poor. He'd work for a couple of days to buy his cigars and a shirt or two, but nothing else. Now, what can a girl expect from a man like that?

"Five months later, he fell in love with my adopted sister. He came to ask my permission and said that, if we would continue our friendship, he'd leave her.

" 'Oh, God,' I said, 'please marry her as soon as possible!' Then I said to my sister, because I loved her very much, 'You just got yourself the biggest unhappiness in the world, but it's your taste and his, and may God do his will.' And their happiness was that, as soon as they married, she got pregnant. She looked like a big jug. After six months, she died because he didn't take care of her.

"And then there was this widower who came back to court me again. Chased me up and down the slopes. When he was younger I didn't want him, and now, half dead, with a crippled soul, I needed him less. 'Quit fooling yourself,' I'd say. If he cried before, he cried more now.

'But my happiness is with you,' he'd say.

'Happiness,' I replied, 'you won't find with me. I said no, and I mean no!'

"So he married a cousin of mine, and after six months she died. Then he went to Cayey and married again, and that wife died a couple of years ago. She was a big jug!

"I met Rafael working tobacco. He was still a boy, and I hadn't

"I really liked the old days better! You could be garlic-ugly and strong."

fallen in love with him, nor he with me. He'd flatter me (*me echaba flores*) [he threw flowers to me], but, the devil, only flattery! A year after I got rid of Gabino, I was going steady with him [Rafael]. When we had the tobacco dance with the piano, I was engaged to Rafael. My future mother-in-law brought me the invitation, and we all went, my boyfriend, my sister, and my other sister, and me, of course. We danced mazurkas, polkas, *seis gambao, corríos, chor-reaos* until five in the morning. Did we have fun! I never heard such a piano! And if we had fun gathering tobacco, we had more fun that night. After each song we'd have a drink. In those days we had *parrandas*. We'd go in groups and stop at each house, do a few turns and go on to another house with our music, and do a few more turns. We'd keep it up until dawn.

"Today everyone goes to the movies, but I never liked it. Once in my life, I went with my husband. All I saw was streams of ducks, ducks, and more ducks. I said to my husband, 'That's the movies? I'm going home. Ducks I can see at home!' And I never went again." [Doña Lola must have seen a Donald Duck cartoon.]

"I really liked the old days better! It was nice in those days. You could be garlic-ugly and strong. For me there was no right or wrong. I felt I could do anything."

"This plantation has been in our family for a hundred years."

2

Hacienda Roses

The road winds through mountainous country, past spectacular views, eleven miles beyond Utuado, to where a sign nailed to a tree says, "Hacienda Roses." At the end of a narrow dirt road, among trees and tropical flowers, is the home of the Roses family.

Minnie Roses, the daughter of the owners, told us the history of the hacienda.

"This plantation has been in our family for a hundred years. My great grandfather came from Spain and bought property. Like other Spaniards, he established a business and then, in a few months, went back to Spain. He never lived here. The land passed to my grandfather and his brothers, who used it for hunting. Later, it became one of the biggest coffee plantations on the Island—3,000 acres. Sometimes grandfather would come to oversee and to hunt, but he lived in Utuado, later in Arecibo and San Juan.

"My grandfather graduated from medical school in Spain, but, before beginning his practice, he went to take special courses in Maryland. On the trip to America, he met my grandmother, who was part English and Canadian. That's why I'm called Minnie instead of María Teresa, which is my real name. They fell in love on the ship and, after a lot of opposition from her family, they married. She never learned to speak Spanish well. She was one of the most beautiful ladies in Puerto Rico. At the balls, she was usually elected beauty queen!

"In Maryland my grandfather met President Theodore Roosevelt on a hunting trip, and they became friends. Once the President sent grandfather a telegram saying that he was coming to Puerto Rico.

"Grandfather mounted his horse and started across the river to greet the President. Crossing from the other side, the President's car began to sputter, frightening the horse. Grandfather fell into the river, and the President had to help him out. So that nothing like that would happen again, the President promised to have a bridge built over the river, the Río Grande in Utuado. It is called *Puente de Miguelito* (Miguelito's Bridge) in honor of my grandfather.

"My grandfather was the first doctor in Puerto Rico to treat cancer with radium. He and his colleagues were also pioneers in anemia and parasite research."

Señora Roses, the mother, remarked: "The people here used to go barefoot, they were so poor. They walked in the mud, and their feet were swollen from the parasites. It was very painful, and my father and Bailey Ashford found a treatment for it, a vaccine."

Minnie: "Yes! Ashford was an American doctor, a colonel in the Spanish-American War, but he lived here in Puerto Rico. An avenue in San Juan is named after him. He and my grandfather were friendly with all the English and Americans who lived in Puerto Rico then.

"In 1945, my father inherited the plantation and fell in love with it. He had been a dandy in San Juan, coming to the country only on picnics, but soon he wanted no more weekends or partying in San Juan. He came to live here and built this house.

"He loved this place so much, he got involved in landscaping and botany. He did the landscaping at the International Airport in San Juan. Imagine, a man who knew nothing about plants, agriculture, or land!

"This region is called Don Alonzo after the first Indian chief baptized here. There is a big Indian cave nearby. My uncle, Dr. José Oliver, an archaeologist at the Institute of Culture, has located an ancient Indian cemetery and ball park.

"In 1945, some old people here had never seen a car. One day, my mother and I went to San Juan to buy a red power wagon. When we came up the road, people fell to their knees, then they ran to warn my father that a monster was coming up the hill!

"Many places in Puerto Rico didn't have electricity or running water. Our old hacienda had no bath, only an outhouse. About ten years ago, my father built the road leading to the hacienda. Before that, we'd leave our car where the main road ended, about 12

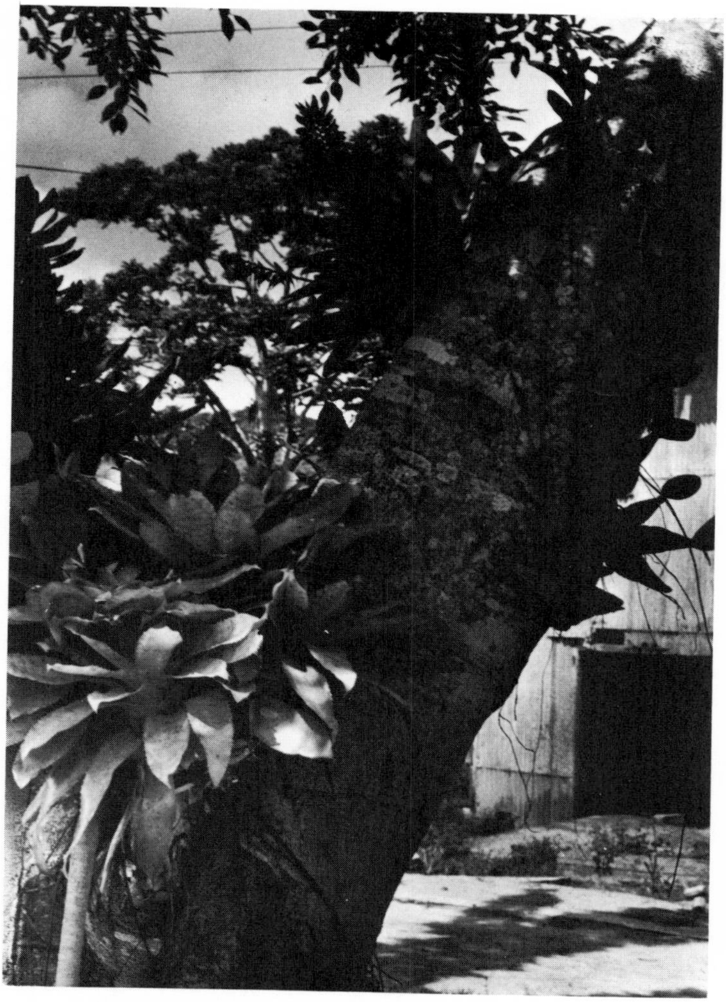

"My father loved this place so much he got involved in landscaping and botany."

kilometers [7½ miles] from here, and come the rest of the way by horse, an hour's ride!"

Señora Roses: "We once had several haciendas. This one had about fifty families, and we knew everyone. There's an old man here who is a hundred and fifteen years old. And he still walks up and down these hills, chewing tobacco!"

The Roses family is nostalgic about its happier past, when the plantation was prosperous and many of Puerto Rico's popular leaders were entertained at the hacienda. Señor Roses was one of the founders of the Popular Democratic Party.

Minnie: "My father was an intimate friend of Muñoz Marín, whose father, Muñoz Rivera, our national hero, was a deputy to the *Cortes* in Spain and fought for Puerto Rican autonomy.

"Muñoz Marín lived in New York for many years and, when he came back, he started a political movement and became governor. He had a great gift of speech but didn't want glory or money. When his term as governor ended in 1956, he was as poor as when he came in! The people wanted him to stay on, but he felt he was too old. When he was governor, he would move his staff up here and work

"My uncle . . . has located an ancient Indian cemetery and ball park."

for weeks. The helicopter flew back and forth, bringing his secretaries and aides, typewriters and dictating machines. He loved children and they would jump all over him and he would smile.

Señora Roses: "He loved to come here to rest, because, he said, 'Right now I am on the earth, in this world, but when I walk fifty steps out to the terrace, I feel I am in heaven, in another world, closer to God.' He is a very great poet, and a philosopher."

Señora Roses turned from reminiscence to some observations about local people.

"In the old days, Spanish farmers settled in the mountains. They married Indians, as you can see by the faces of many people here. The colored people have come just lately, mainly from the coast, where their ancestors were slaves in the sugar-cane plantations. In this area, there is little mixture with blacks."

"Many of the poor are spiritualists and use herbs and prayers as cures. Women still give birth assisted by an herb-doctor, usually a woman. In serious cases they sometimes call in a *chisso* [witch or conjurer]."

Minnie described the problems of growing coffee in Puerto Rico.

"At first, we had about 500 acres of coffee. We have had to reduce that amount every year. We don't have enough workers. We can't compete with factory wages. That's why the plantations are slowly disappearing.

"Coffee is expensive because of the middlemen. They make the big profits, not the plantation-owners. Coffee loses weight as it dries, but we have to pay the pickers for the original weight. Coffee is very delicate. If it rains too much, the blossoms fall and there is less coffee. If it doesn't rain enough, there are fewer blossoms and less coffee. If there is too much rain, when the berry is green, it ripens all at once, falls to the ground, and there is not enough time to pick it. If it rains when the coffee is ripe, it falls to the ground and much is lost.

"Puerto Rican coffee costs a dollar a pound in San Juan and 85 cents in New York, because it goes to the States first and then comes back to us. We have to pay the same as if it weren't Puerto Rican coffee!

"Before coffee is ready to drink, it goes through many processes. Coffee blooms three or four times from January to May, when the biggest blooming takes place and the tiny green beans come out and start growing. By September, the beans are ready to be picked.

Not all the bushes ripen at the same time, and picking time lasts about three months. My mother and father used to put the pickers in one area, and when that was done, they moved to another.

"The ripe coffee bean (a red berry) is shelled in a machine we have right here. Then it is washed, and the dust, straw, and external particles are scrubbed from the beans. Then the coffee is taken out of the tank to dry.

"There are two ways to dry coffee—in a drying cylinder or by spreading the beans out in a shed. The second way takes three or four weeks because it rains a lot during picking time. In the drying machine, the coffee dries in thirty-six hours. We used to have a big cylinder when the plantation was in full production. We dried 8,000 pounds at a time. When the plantation size was reduced, my father sold the cylinder to a big company. So now we dry it in the shed. Sometimes we sell it green after it's picked.

"After the coffee is dried, it has to be husked. Then you roast it. That's when the aroma comes out. It doesn't smell like coffee before that. The berry tastes a little like peaches.

"When business got bad, we added a bath and a few rooms to our original building and opened a guest house. We needed money and also wanted to give employment to the workers still living here on the plantation."

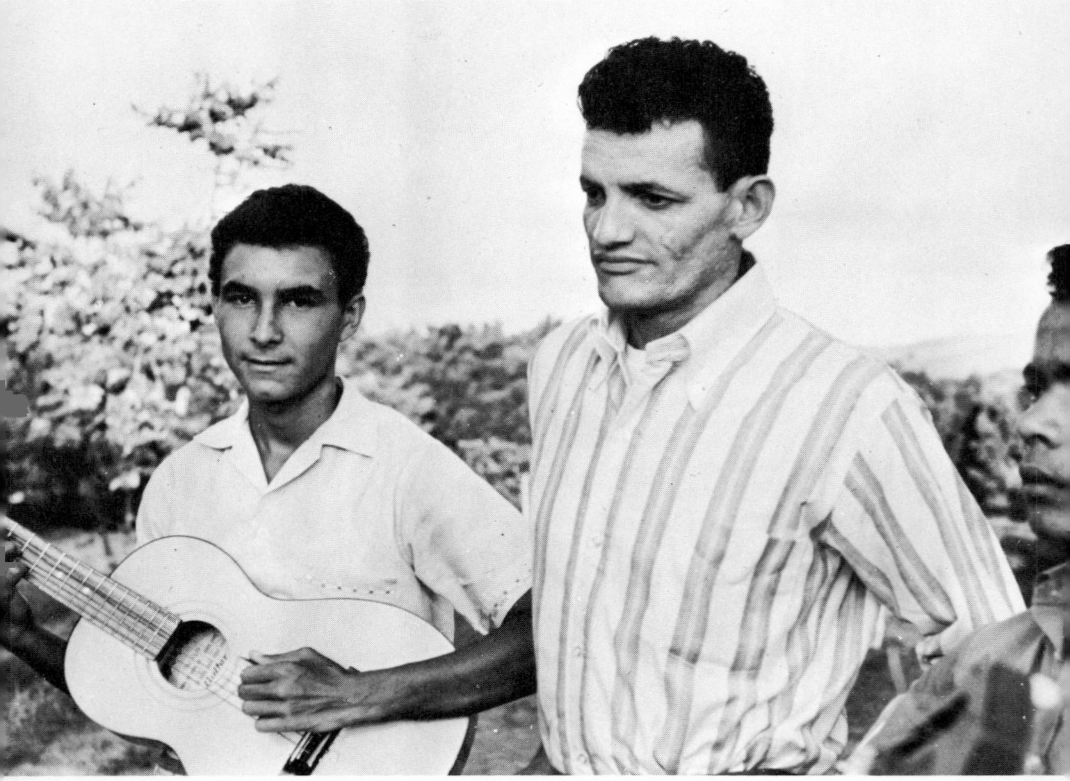

And if there is a little guitar
I also sing my song
And if I get a nickel
I spend it on billiards.

3

Songs and *Santos*

In the mountains, Spanish traditions prevail despite the impact of urban radio and television. Among the *jíbaros,* as country people are called, are gifted musician-poets famous for their ability to compose extemporaneously on any theme—politics, religion, love. Some of the best *jíbaros,* though they are illiterate, are very wise and have a great knowledge of life and a remarkable memory for events. During World War II, the news of the day was sung on a San Juan radio station by Jesús El de Bayamón [Jesús, the One from Bayamón]. Even now, several radio stations employ similarly gifted singing poets.

The following song was composed by Luis Marcano, a young singer who lives in complete obscurity on a mountain farm near Cidra. It is a *décima,* a ten-line verse form of Spanish origin.

Le, lo, le, le, lo, le,
no tengo nada que hacer;
no tengo nada que hacer;
en esta vida tengo que seguir
porque para mi es un placer;
todo lo puedo tener.
No me tengo que ahorrar,
yo no tengo en que pensar;
este systema nos ama;
yo tengo todo a la mano
sin tener que trabajar.

Le, lo, le, le, lo, le,
me levanto como a las diez;
me tiro la ropa encima,
luego voy a la cocina,
tengo el almuerzo y el café
y luego como a las tres
un baño me voy a dar;
y vuelta me pongo a dar
hacia abajo y hacia arriba;
y así paso mi vida
sin tener que trabajar.

Le, lo, le, le, lo, le,
me meto en vasilón;
me meto en vasilón;
me tomo la cervecita,
y si estará guitarrita,
también canto mi canción
y si consigo el vellón
yo lo juego en billar,
puedo perder o ganar
porqué voy a enfurecerme,
si lo mío es entretenerme
sin tener que trabajar.

Le, lo, le, le, lo, le,
yo tengo una madrecita
yo tengo una madrecita
ella es mi madre adorada
que me pone en la semana
mi ropa bien planchadita,
si no me lo hace mi hermanita,
no la tengo que ahorrar,
no lo tengo que mandar,
para que voy a insistir,
si así yo puedo vivir
sin que tengo que trabajar.

Le, lo, le, le, lo, le,
I have nothing to do,
I have nothing to do,

In this life I must go on
Because for me it is a pleasure.
I can have everything.
I don't have to save.
I have nothing on my mind.
This system loves us.
I have everything at hand
Without having to work.

Le, lo, le, le, lo, le,
I arise at about ten.
I throw my clothes around.
Then I go to the kitchen,
I have lunch and coffee,
And then about three
I take a bath.
I go for a walk
To the bottom and up to the top,
And that's how my life goes,
Without having to work.

Le, lo, le, le, lo, le,
I have become a wastrel.
I have become a wastrel.
I drink my little beer,
And if there is a little guitar,
I also sing my song,
And if I get a nickel,
I spend it on billiards.
I can lose or win
Why should I be mad—
If I can entertain myself
Without having to work?

Le, lo, le, le, lo, le,
I have a little mother.
She is my adored mother,
And every week she sets out
My clothes well ironed.
If not, my little sister does it.
I don't have to spare her.

I don't have to order her.
Why should I insist,
If I can live like this,
Without having to work.

The following *décima* was composed by Modesto Torres after the assassination of President Kennedy on November 22, 1963. Torres is known as El Jíbaro Orocoveño [The Jíbaro from Orocovis].

Hoy el Presidente ha muerto
deja el Pueblo Americano
y a todo el linaje humano
en sentimientos envuelto;
parecía no era cierto
lo surgido de repente
desde oriente hasta Occidente;
quedó el mundo confundido
al saber que ha fallecido,
el más joven Presidente

Cuando se verificaba
que había muerto se decía
toda la Ciudadania
muy pesarosa quedaba;
el público atento estaba
lamentando hondamente
muy desesperadamente,
sintió al Paladín grandioso
era el hombre más valioso
y el más joven Presidente

El 22 de noviembre
una mano criminal
con un arma Infernal
quitó la vida a este hombre;
queda en la historia su nombre
y en la humanidad latente
su espíritu diariamente
vivirá en la raza humana
la Nación Americana
pierde a un joven Presidente

Cuando a Puerto Rico vino
todo el pueblo lo esperaba
porqué el pueblo lo admiraba
y lo seguía en su camino;
Kennedy hombre muy fino,
decidido y complaciente,
habló con todo la gente;
la misma me ha preguntado
porqué ha sido asesinado
este joven Presidente

Today the President has died.
He leaves the American people
And the entire human lineage
Enveloped in sentiments.
It seemed it was not true.
It swept suddenly
From the east to the west.
The world remained confused
To learn that he had fallen,
The youngest President.

When it was verified
That he had died, it is said
That all citizens
Were left very sorrowful.
The public was heedful,
Lamenting deeply,
Very desperately,
Feeling the grand champion
Was the most valuable man
And the youngest President.

The twenty-second of November,
A criminal hand
With an infernal weapon
Took away the life of this man.
In history his name remains,
And in latent humanity
His spirit daily
Will live on in the human race.

The American Nation
Lost a young President.

When he came to Puerto Rico
All the people awaited him
Because the people admired him
And followed him on his road.
Kennedy, a very fine man,
Determined and agreeable,
Spoke with all the people.
The same ones have asked me
Why he was assassinated,
This young President.

During the nineteenth century, the making of *santos,* small wooden household saints, exquisitely carved and painted, was a popular art in Puerto Rico. Mainly through efforts of the Institute of Puerto Rican Culture, many old *santos* have been collected in villages and towns throughout the island in recent years.

Norberto Cedeño, one of the last great *santo*-makers, lives in Toa Alta, a small town near Arecibo. In 1969, the white-haired Don Norberto, who was born in 1897, was still spry, inspired, busy, and cheerful, despite the obvious poverty of his circumstances. His little wooden house, half workshop and half bedroom, overlooks a quiet, lovely valley. All around the small shop are the tools of his trade: cans of paint, glue, and *santos* in various stages of completion. "I've been making *santos* for twenty-three years. Before that, I used to do commercial work—painting scenery, sculpturing marble angels for cemeteries, and engraving tombstones in high and low relief.

"I have dedicated my life to making *santos* because I suffered a very big accident. I was painting a big sign when the ladder collapsed and I fell to the pavement. My right leg was fractured. The doctor did a good job and, when I saw that my leg didn't end up in a trash can, I devoted myself to this work. That's the way I give thanks. I'm not as crippled as I might have been and it hurts a bit, but at least I'm not on crutches.

"People come here from many places to buy my saints. Sometimes I make a saint for my neighbors; they appreciate that, but mostly I work for the Institute of Culture. I send them to Señor Ricardo Alegría [director of the Institute], and Walter Murray

"My favorite saints
are San Antonio,
the Virgin of Carmen,
the Miraculous One,
Jesus Christ, and
the Lonely Soul. . . .
My God, she's the
last word in saints."

Chiesa [director of the Institute's Center of Popular Arts] writes articles about my saints. They have been exhibited at fairs in Ponce, Mayagüez, and Barranquitas.

"My favorite saints are San Antonio, the Virgin of Carmen, the Miraculous One, Jesus Christ, and the Lonely Soul (*Ánima Sola*). My God, she's the last word in saints—that's the one that defends women. If some woman has a husband who is a bit perverse—well, that's the saint for it. She makes miracles but demands payment. She's not fussy; she takes all kinds of payments. If you light an oil lamp or four or five candles, it's the same to her. But, if a woman doesn't pay, she'll never let her alone—won't let her sleep.

"If your husband is running around with other women—as it happens, because husbands like to dilly-dally once in a while, right? —we cheat a bit. The woman calls on her *Ánima Sola.* All she has to do is stamp on the floor three times, hard as hell, and say, "*Ánima Sola,* stop him from whatever he is doing and drag him here!" And he has to leave wherever he is and come to her. Yes, I love that little animal [the saint]; it does us men harm, but it's really miraculous! Us poor men, we're really like that, but we should keep our women in good condition and not fool around!"

"Us poor men . . . we should keep our women in good condition and not fool around!"

4

Loíza Aldea

CASTOR AYALA

Loíza Aldea, located on the North Shore, is the only Negro village of Puerto Rico. Long isolated from the rest of the Island, the village developed its own customs and traditions, which are part Spanish, part African. In 1935, the old, sandy oxcart trail built by the Spaniards was finally paved. For the first time, Loíza was united with the main highway, which runs the length of the Island. Despite modernization, many of the old ways are still proudly preserved by the villagers.

Five miles away are the barrios Alta and Baja Medianías, considerably poorer and even more devoted to their past than Loíza Aldea. Until a generation ago, Medianías barely subsisted on small-scale farming, fishing, and part-time sugar-plantation work. Today, factory and construction work has brought financial improvement. Refrigerators, washing machines, and, above all, television are found everywhere, even in some of the poorest huts.

The older part of Medianías is a vast coconut grove, with huts scattered among the huge trees that provide shade from the blazing sun; colorful flower gardens and potted plants contrast with the dilapidated condition of many huts. Small children play naked in the clearings, watched over by their older sisters and brothers.

Along the main street, the highway through town, are bars, restaurants, small grocery stores, and dance halls. Closer to the seashore, on small plots of land with no trees, are modern cement houses equipped with car-port, running water, and gas stove.

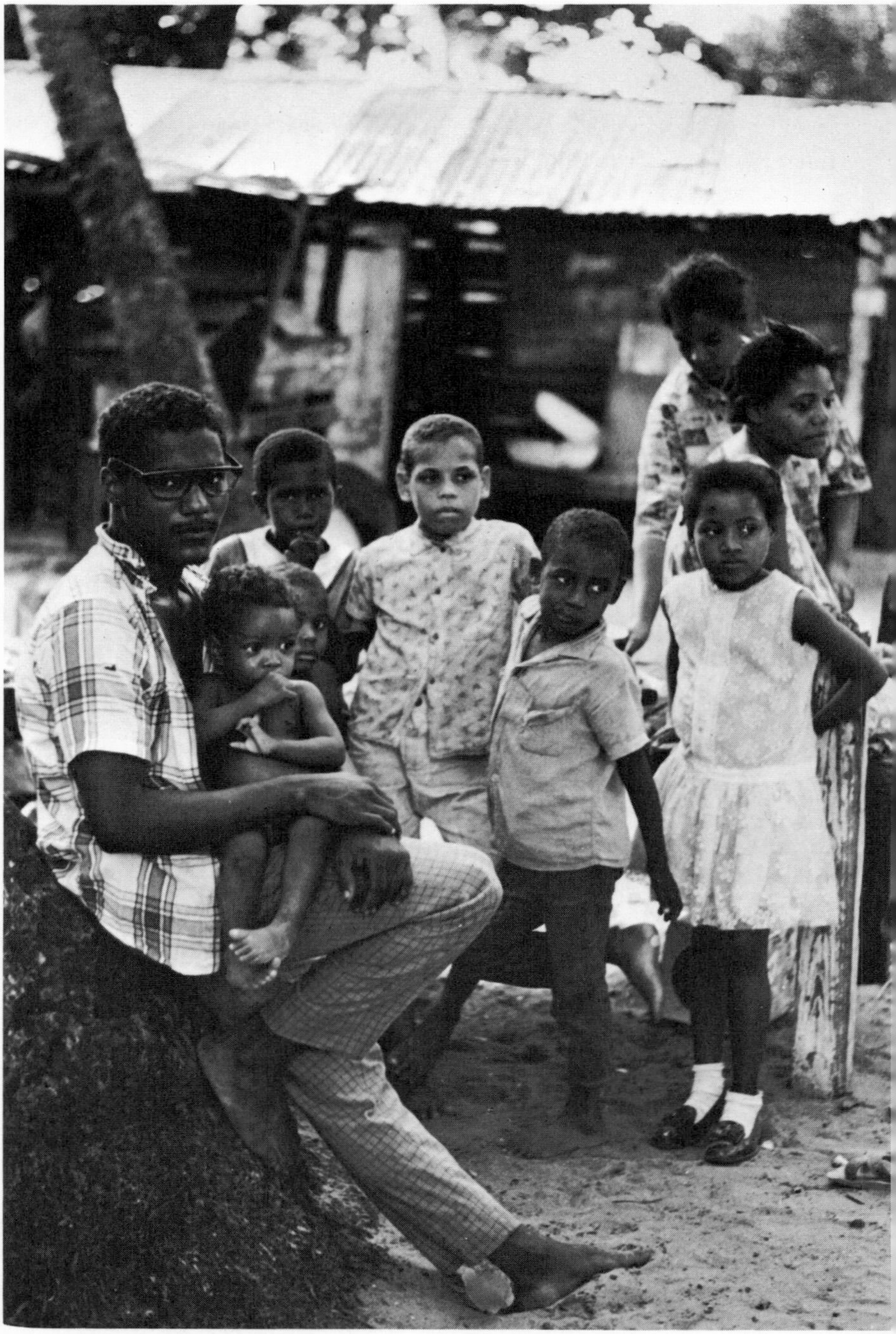

"Nobody here is pure black. There are many mixes. . . . Nobody can say, 'I am pure.'"

Churches of all denominations abound: Catholic, Pentecostal, Jehovah's Witnesses, Baptist. Any home in Medianías, famous for its spiritualists, might be used for meetings and seances.

Castor Ayala is one of the most respected citizens of Medianías. His wares and his fame as mask-maker and handcraftsman are known far beyond the village. Speaking in English, he said, "I never studied high school. My father was too poor to send me." As a youth, he worked in sugar-cane fields near Loíza, and he is still proud of his reputation as a hard worker. Now he has a workshop, where he makes many articles of coconut—candy dishes, cups, candle-holders, ship models. He also paints local landscapes and creates fanciful birds of wood, coconut husks, and turkey feathers. His wife sells homemade candies and pineapple ices.

"I started painting when I was a kid," recalls Mr. Ayala. "My father couldn't buy me paints, so I squeeze the colors from leaves and flowers and use the point of a feather for a brush. At first, I painted designs on a coconut flowerpot we had in the classroom. The teacher liked it and she order a dozen more. Then I sold six or seven in Río Grande, a town near here. During vacation I went to San Juan, and the souvenir stores ordered me to make three dozen. Wow! They were crazy about them! Afterwards, I copy

"I never studied high school. My father was too poor to send me."

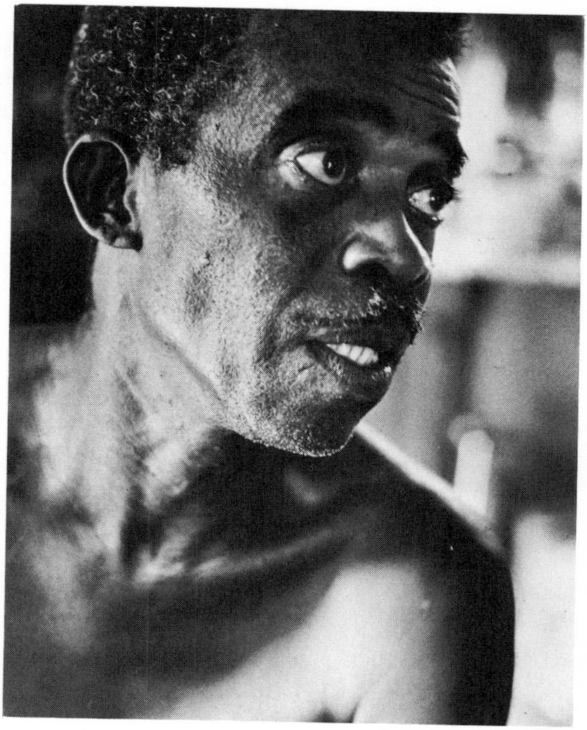

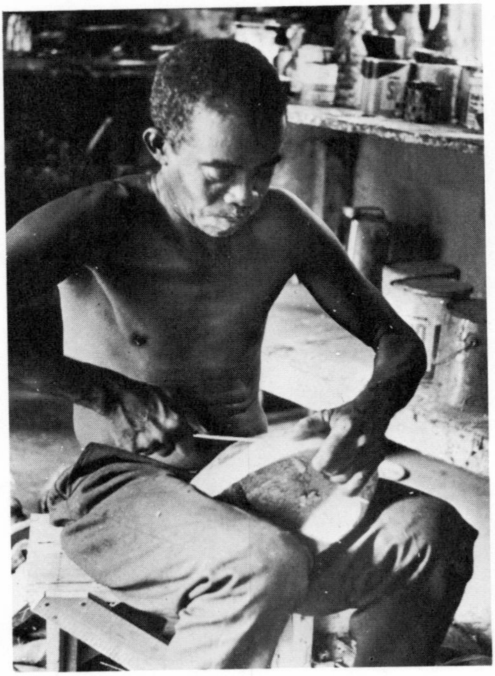

"I picked the biggest coconut I could find."

other things in my father's house. Here we have a custom to keep articles from ancient times as a *recuerdo* [souvenir]. I copied coffee cups and children's banks—everything made of coconut and roots. Now I make thirty-two different articles."

Every day, Señor Ayala, his captain's hat set jauntily on his head, wheels his bicycle down the road to his workshop in the coconut grove. The cutting and sawing are done by machine, but the rest is handwork. His workers do routine tasks; Ayala does the delicate and artistic work. He sits outdoors under huge fruit trees, surrounded by husks, and talks to visitors as he designs the masks or cuts them from the soft coconut husks. These masks are used during fiesta times.

"My second [great] grandfather gave me a piece of a mask that was so old it crumpled in my fingers. I think it was used when the festival began, around 1830. I saw another old mask in the house of a friend. The colors were nearly erased, so I washed it, guessed the colors, and designed new masks."

Many villagers made their own masks but, since 1936, Señor Ayala has been the principal mask-maker. Once a British admiral ordered a mask from him. "I picked the biggest coconut I could

"The colors were nearly erased, so I washed it, guessed the colors, and designed new masks."

find. The mask was grotesque but the best I ever made. Three months later, the admiral—(he had a monocle)—came to see me. 'Ayala,' he said, 'you know where is your mask? It is here.' And he showed me a postcard of a place in England. 'Where is that?' I ask. 'It is the receiving room of Buckingham Palace. And it is written on the bottom who made it, and what it means.' I was very proud! From that time on, I have been very busy. I can't get a vacation because there is too much work."

Señor Ayala has workers not only in the shop but all over the village. They work at home and each weekend deliver the articles for payment.

Señor Ayala believes he has an invisible protector who always stands guard at his shop and is the source of his inspiration. "One morning, about five o'clock, my neighbor saw an Indian standing at the gate, his hands across his chest. He was smoking a pipe and had great feathers in the back of his head and part of his head shaved. She called her sister, and she saw the same thing. They couldn't work that day, because they were shaking and had a fever

"They told me and I joked, 'Ha, don't worry. That's my watch man, don't get afraid.' Then I went to Guayama, and the spiritualist there say she see the same thing. About five different ladies [spiritualists] in different parts of the island say the same. One of them told me 'the Indian was your father in ancient times, and he is by your side always. . . . Don't you feel him by your side when you are alone?' 'Yes,' I said, 'I don't see him, but I feel him there.' She said, 'Everything you design is not from you; your hand is directed by him.' Perhaps she is right, because I feel something rare when I design. I have to design the moment I see it, or I forget it."

According to Señor Ayala, Medianías was a small Indian village when the Spaniards arrived. "The village grew gently, but many relics prove the Indians lived on one side and the Spaniards and other people on the other. Then the blacks came." Señor Ayala still remembers stories his grandparents told him about slavery, when black men were beaten by the Spaniards, but he also recalls, "My second grandfather told me the Spaniards like very much the black race and they mix the race. That's the reason in Puerto Rico there is no pure black. Nobody here is pure black. There are many mixes, Spanish race, Indian race, and black race. Nobody can say 'I am pure.' If one say that, I say, 'Where is your grandfather and your second grandmother?' Everywhere there is a mixture! . . .

"And that is the reason there is no racial problem. We live like brothers. We can stay in any hotel, and they don't refuse to receive us because is black, is white."

Señor Ayala feels comfortable with people of all races and with rich and poor, when he is on his own home ground. "I have been with rich, with poor. I knew a millionaire, pure Spanish. He came here and stay with me, and we go to drink beer, and he make me go in his car. Punch! and the door open. Punch! the door close. Another switch and the glass go up! Another switch—the car open! He have to do nothing. We go to the restaurant, but I don't feel comfortable, because, eh, it is very *lujoso* [luxurious]. He told me, 'Ayala, please feel at home here!' but . . . I like the country. Here we feel happy like the birds in the skies. No troubles, no fears—we live in the open air. In the city, we live like in a jail. My son and my daughter work in the city, but they come home every night, no matter the hour. I have growed them in a way that they love the country. Here we hold the customs and the feeling of our forefathers. In the city we lose everything."

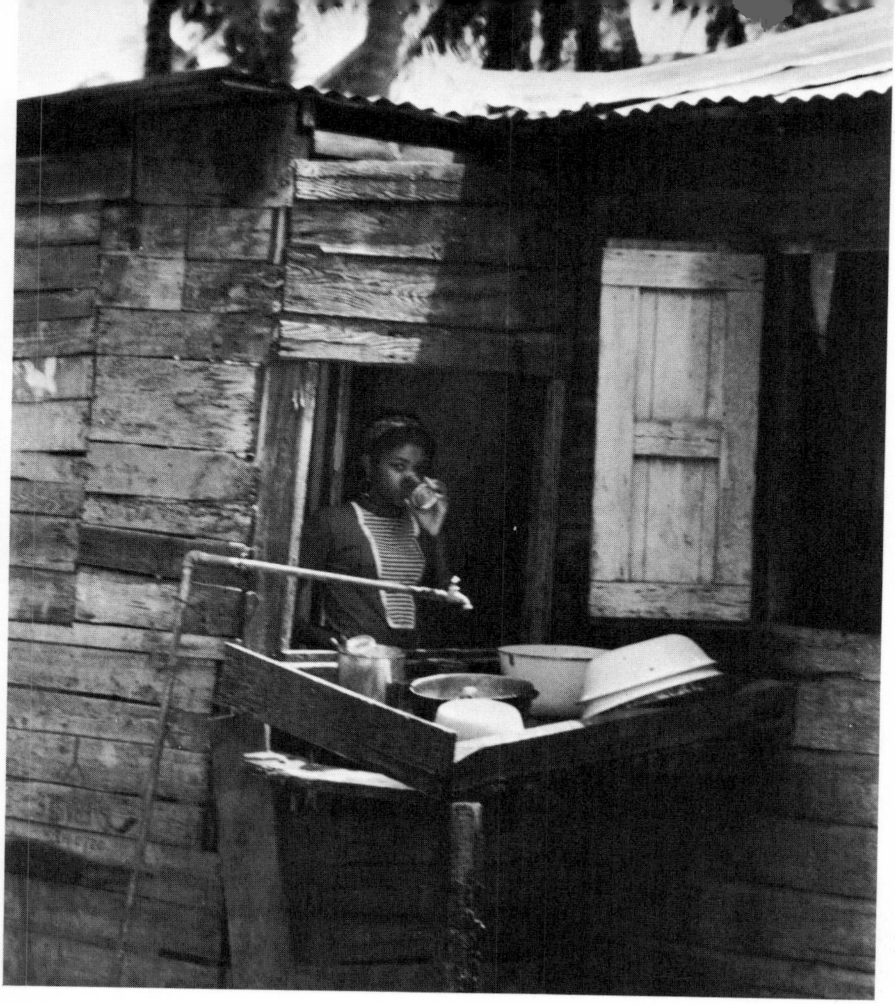

Modern improvements have trickled into Loíza, but Señor Ayala is not convinced the people are happier.

Reminiscing about life in the village when he was growing up, Señor Ayala told us of a courtship custom:

"When a boy went to ask for the hand of a lady, he must place a stake with his name on it in her yard. If the father take the stake out of the yard—finished! That family don't want him! If the father place it on the door, that mean he can come inside. That is true; I saw it!

"But, before the boy is accepted, he must prove himself by fighting the father. No real, real fight, not to kill, but to show he is strong enough to defend his bride!

"If the girl was interested, she would sit on a special bench in her yard. This mean a warning to other boys to stay away. Once the boy and girl are engaged, she don't do this anymore. Even today, we call these benches *espantanovios* [suitor-frighteners]."

The children of Loíza live out of doors most of the time, in an atmosphere of freedom. Children of all ages play together, swim in blue-green, sunlit waters, and romp along sandy beaches lined with coconut palms.

Señor Ayala: "When I was a boy, the little children had no cover, just as they were born, no shirts, and barefoot. Until eight years old, they wore no pants. Mothers made rag dolls for the girls. The boys make cars with a long stick and wheels from the covers of cans.

"I remember girls and boys taking a bath when it rained. They run to the plants and take the drops of rain on them. And when the rain passed, they go to the house and dry themselves.

"But, in the house, it was nearly a military discipline. We must be inside at eight o'clock—after eight we are punished. And they spank us with a long belt, no matter a boy or girl, who don't obey immediately. And eating, they have an hour, six o'clock, exactly at six!

"The man was boss. He ordered everything. The mother had to obey since he earned the money. But, today, the lady earns money, and both of them have authority in the house. Many women today have more authority—it's going in reverse.

"I don't like it as it is today. I order in my house just as my forefathers did. When I step hard on the floor [here Señor Ayala accompanied his words with actions], my children say, 'Father don't like something here. He is stamping his feet on the floor!' Then I say, 'This and this and this is not good,' and they immediately correct what is wrong. They obey. As you see, my boys are polite because I educate them like my father did me. I don't want my boys and girls outside at night. Freddy is fourteen—he must be at home by eight. Raul is twenty-one; he is a man now, and he is free of our power. I like to have my kids around me, but they are like the birds. When they were little *pichones* [pigeons], they stay with us, but immediately they are older, they fly away and they leave me alone.

"When I was young, Loíza looked like a real jungle. Each house was about one or two kilometers from the other. The things in the houses were primitive because people keep the customs of their

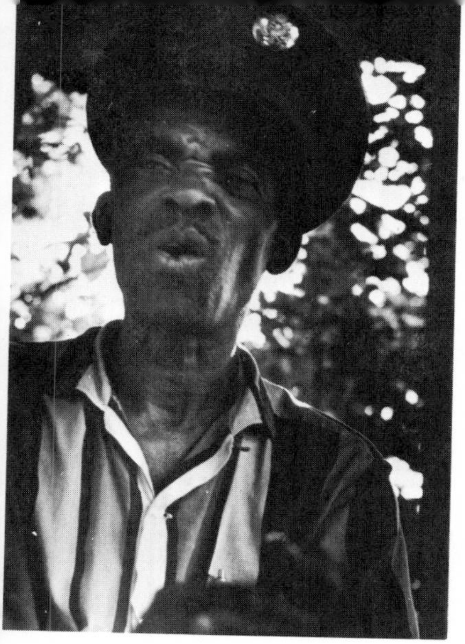

*"The man was boss. . . .
the mother had to obey,
since he earned the money."*

forefathers. Dishes were made of wood and the cups of coconut or bamboo. There were no forks, only spoons of coconut. They were completely black. For cooking they bought plain kettles from the highlands. They were good! The big dishes were for the father and mother, and the smaller ones for the kids, according to their age. From 1925, they begin to disappear because we receive pots from the States and the people find them better.

"In ancient times, the houses were made of palm. The roof was palm leaves, and the walls and floors were boards of royal palm. They get a nice black color, very polished, by themselves, and never get termites!

*"Don't you feel him
by your side
when you are alone?"*

"There was no electric light, no electric kitchens, no stove. You had three stones and a kettle. Three stones to place the kettle on and fire it. That was the kitchen.

"Some people were so poor, they could not afford to eat every meal, despite low prices. Sometimes we went to school without lunch. On Saturdays my family ate two meals of coffee and bread but nothing for lunch."

By 1940, modern improvements began to trickle into Loíza, but Señor Ayala is not convinced that people are happier. "You look back to 1940. The people here were in better condition. They didn't have so many possessions, and they were more content with themselves."

Medianías runs along the sea. Before the dam was built, the Río Grande used to overflow its banks. The villagers fear hurricanes, but the big blows seldom come near the Island. Good storytellers like Señor Ayala, however, love to talk about those that did strike the area. The children gather around him to hear the awesome tales.

"The hurricane of San Cipriano," he begins, fixing his bulging eyes on the children's upturned faces, "was in 1932. She had winds 180 miles in speed. That night the wind blew in gusts. We had no warning, but we knew a hurricane was coming because the goats sniffed the sky at about five o'clock and were very nervous. My father say, 'You see the goats; there is going to be a hurricane today.'

"We take the goats to the yard and tie them up, but they don't want to stay, so we untie them and they run under the house.

"We know it by the hens too. The hens here in this country sleep in the trees, but not that evening. Mother say, 'Oh, look! They are going under the floor, one after the other, whoooop, under the floor.' Instinctively, they were searching for a safer place.

"Father say there will be a hurricane in two or three hours. We prepared everything neatly. Every window was locked with a board, all the beds wrapped and tied. We leave nothing loose. By six or seven o'clock, the wind strike harder. Father say the hurricane is about half an hour away.

"We work harder and harder. We could see nothing—it was nearly night. Then father tie us with a big rope one to another, one to another. By nine o'clock, the roof was stretching. I said, 'Father, let's get out of the house; it is going to fall down!' When the last one—that was father—got outside, the roof fell down—crash!—

"My boys are polite because I educate them like my father did me."

inside the house. If we didn't go out, the house could have killed us all.

"Till five in the morning, we stay outside. The hurricane swept over us; we see raining and balls of fire around the trees, balls of fire in the wind. We were wet and trembling with the wind and the sand that blew, with the wind that burned your face. Wow! The palm trees around the house fall down.

"When the hurricane was over, we try to go inside the house, but we can't. Then we saw the lamplight. You see, when the roof fall down, it collapsed in the center of the house but left the corners standing. During all the hurricane, the lamp stayed burning!

"When the storm was over, I start to make breakfast for all the families whose houses fall down. Most of the village was down.

"After that hurricane, we moved away from the seashore to where we are now. The winds of a hurricane sound like two hundred airplanes at the same time."

Loíza Aldea is a sleepy town most of the year but, late in July, it comes to life for a week of celebration in honor of Santiago [Saint James], its patron saint.

Castor Ayala: "People here wait the whole year for the coming of the festival. They prepare their best suits; the best foods and the houses are prepared with new chairs, new utensils. Even the little kids are in the road to see the masks and parade. They dance, too. Yeah, we feel it in the blood! Many people wait to be married or baptize the children during the fiesta because it is an *ocasíon.* Our fiesta is a mixture of religious festival and carnival, and it is traditional in my home town.

"This festival of Santiago originated in Spain. One evening, there was a great battle between the Spaniards and Moors, and the Spaniards wanted to win before sunset. So they made big masks with horns, like the ones in our festival, and costumes like a vampire bat, like a devil in colors. Then they placed soldiers in the costumes and sent them at the head of the Spanish Army. When the Moors saw those devils jumping around, they get afraid and run away. In the confusion, the Spanish Army attack and won the battle before sunset. It was Santiago who led the Spanish soldiers to victory.

"About 1832, an old woman here found a statue in the trunk of a tree in Medianías. She showed it to the priest. He said it was the statue of Santiago. He put it in the church. The next day, the statue was back in the trunk of the tree. Then he took it back to the church and told everybody it was a miracle. He make a Mass and a procession around the town plaza and from the tree to the church. Every year since then, they make a festival in honor of Santiago, and then make a procession from the tree in Medianías to the church in Loíza Aldea.

"In the festival, the masks with the big horns means the Devil against the Christians. We call them *vejigantes*. The screen-masks and costumes in color means the Spanish *caballeros* that fight against the Moors. Our festival has a big taste of Spanish history."

The *bomba* is one of the highlights of the fiesta. Every night, often until dawn, Medianías resounds with the hypnotic rhythm of drums, undulating dance, and melodious song. The rhythm starts, and people of all ages appear from the dark grove to form a circle around the drummers. The drums begin—then, a solo dancer steps into the center of the ring, jumping, shaking, and twisting his body until he is thoroughly exhausted; all the while, the villagers sing traditional verses:

El Rabo de la Cometa	The Tail of the Kite
Una vieja camisa se levantó *y el rabo de la cometa se la llevó.*	An old shirt was lifted up, And the tail of a kite took it away.
Si la quieres ver *levántate temprano y la verás*	If you want to see it, Get up early and you will see it.
Dolores	
Dónde esta Dolores *para bailar, Dolores!* *Ay, búscame a Dolores.* *para bailar, Dolores!*	Where is Dolores? Let's dance, Dolores! Oh, I look for Dolores. Let's dance, Dolores!
Ron, Ron	Rum, Rum
Ron, ron, pido yo *anís, anís de Corazón.* *Si no hay anís* *que venga ron.*	Rum, rum, I beg of you, Anise, anise of Corazón. If there is no anise, Let there be rum.

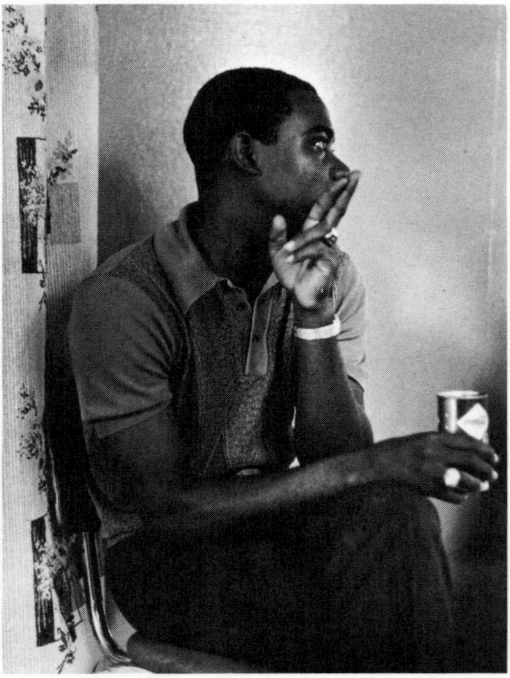

"Raul is twenty-one, he is a man, now."

Good dancers and drummers are the pride of the village, and all, including young children, are encouraged to participate. The Ayalas are the only family, however, that has professional status: they perform at the theater of the Institute of Culture in San Juan, on television, and occasionally in other cities on the island.

Señor Ayala's son Marcos, who works in the television industry in San Juan but lives in Loíza, relates the following incident:

"Once we were contracted by a bank in Guayama to put on a *bomba*. Little by little, the workers got up and danced around the place. Do you know what happened? Well, there had been a long drought that year but, when we began to play, the clouds gathered above us and the rain came pouring down. 'Oh,' everybody shouted, 'you brought us the rain!' They even wanted to take us to Ponce [an hour away], where it hadn't rained either, but it was too late, and we had a three-hour trip back to Loíza! Sometimes I wonder what would have happened had we played in Ponce!"

Castor Ayala: "When I was seven years old, my grandfather told me many tales of the fiesta. I remember them yet because I have a good mind. He told me that, when the *vejigantes* started from the town, they were very drunk. Everybody get afraid of them. In the old days, there was always two or three fights, and people liked that. They said that the fiesta was no good if they had no fights. Today the fiesta must be peaceful. If there is one or three fights, then it is no good."

After the procession is over, the masqueraders wander through the streets, acting out their parts and asking the onlookers for money. "Please, please," says one man, trying to keep the pillow under his shirt from falling down, "I'm pregnant, take me to Bronx Hospital!" A transvestite, lavishly dressed in a ruffled Spanish dancer's costume, careens down the road, snapping his fingers at the crowd. Two children, wearing stocking masks with holes cut out for eyes and mouth, beg for pennies: "*Somos locos* [we are crazy]," they say as they approach people sitting on their porches.

Several years ago, the Catholic priest of the town, a native-born Spaniard, said, "Loizans are half Christian, half pagan. The Santiago festival is a carnival, not a religious celebration. It is just an excuse for them to drink and dance and have a good time. To be a real Catholic, one must attend Mass. But most of them don't, and even fewer go to confession. Of course I say Mass the opening day of the fiesta. Many priests in Puerto Rico close church doors during fiesta time, but I don't think that's right."

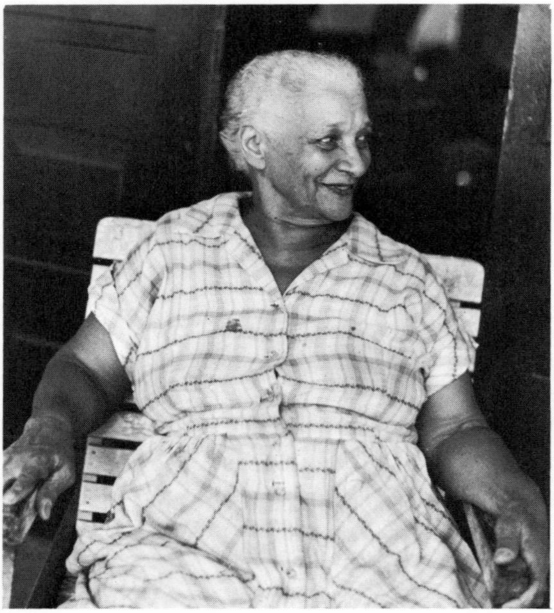

*"Holy Mary,
that was really pretty!
We girls wore a new
dress for each of the
three processions."*

MAÍ VARGAS

Life in Medianías is perhaps best described in the recollections and opinions of its proud elders. The Vargas family has lived in Medianías for many generations, and its members are to be found in many occupations and in economic circumstances from poor to prosperous. The oldest, the peppery grandmother, "Maí" [Mother] Vargas, tells of her early years. Her remarks are translated from the Spanish.

"I was born in Medianías but, when I was eleven years old, my grandparents took me to the church in Loíza Aldea. You just had to be sorry for that town! There were only twenty-two houses scattered here and there and, at night, they were lit by kerosene lamps called *quinqués*. The church was made of wood and the post office of tin and wood, and everything else was *bohíos* [the Indian name for huts]. In those days, the plaza was only a piece of land with four lamp posts. It was grass, not concrete. The goats and cows came to eat there. Imagine, animals eating the grass in the plaza! It was a town that was not a town, but a village—Loíza Aldea—and Medianías was only a humble barrio.

"Today, the new generation makes houses close together but, in those days, if you wanted to talk to people, you had to go right to their houses. You couldn't shout to them, because the houses were too far apart. There were no roads then and no automobiles. People walked or went on horseback. To get to Santurce, you had to go via Boca de Cangrejos [the sandy road along the North Shore]. In order to get there by eleven A.M., you had to start by four in the morning. Two men would go to Fajardo on horseback. One would ride the horse for a while, and then the other, and so on. Life was that way.

"People had little plots of land called *cuerdas* [slightly smaller than an acre], where they planted beans and sweet potatoes. At harvest time, you could sell them at 3 pesos a sack to the buyers who came from Santurce, and then they sold it elsewhere for a *vellón* [a nickel] a pound. And they made a living.

"With corn it was the same way. Holy Mary! They harvested it by the carload. Rice sold for 2 cents a pound. Eggs were half a cent. Later, it went up to 1 cent an egg. People sold cow's milk cheap or gave it to their neighbors or teachers. Those who had money paid 2 cents for a bottle of milk. I had a nanny goat with big teats. I named her Papa, and I raised a daughter of mine on her milk. She filled an oatmeal can in the morning and another in the afternoon!

"Nobody died of hunger. For lack of medicine, perhaps, but not hunger. The neighbors gave food to each other because there was more than enough for everyone.

"In my youth we had schools—the teachers were people who could read and write a little bit, and they taught the others. The parents paid the teachers 75 cents a month for each child. I didn't go to school for very long myself but, like the others, I used to take lunch to the teacher. One day a child would bring corn griddlecakes and milk. Another day, they would take yucca and sweet potato with codfish in oil, or boiled corn—new corn—*sancochoa* [boiled in salt], as they call it in the country, and the teacher would eat it with a bottle of coffee.

"The schools were big huts surrounded by guava and orange trees. We used to play under the trees. We made playing balls from small coconuts and guavas. Sometimes we made jump ropes from the *bejucos* in the palm groves. They are plants that look like rope. I would start jumping—one, two, three, four, five, six, up to ten, and then another girl would jump in my place.

"I was brought up very strictly by my grandparents. I committed an "indiscretion" when I was very young, and my grandfather was so angry that he made me live by myself in a lonely place, not the way I did before—with other boys and girls.

"Later on, I went to visit a neighbor and, on the way, I met this boy and we talked together. When my uncle heard of it, he told my grandma. They held me down and gave me such a spanking I peed in my pants. I was so angry, I ran away. When they missed me that afternoon, they called the police (as if I had really done something terrible). The next day they married us. I had done nothing wrong, and it wasn't until two days later that we really consummated the marriage, thanks to God. I was only seventeen years old, and he was nineteen. I was married by the court, not by the church, because I had committed that indiscretion before.

"We were married for six years and I had four children. Then we were divorced. I lived alone for four years and, during that time, the two older boys died, and the little one of one month and eleven days. Only one little girl remained with me. And that little girl stayed with me even after my new marriage, but she was always more loving toward her father's relatives. She married and died at the age of twenty. A sickness came upon her; she married and she died.

"Then I married this 'blond fellow.' [This was Maí Vargas' little joke, for her husband had very dark skin.] And would you believe it, none of his children had his color. Look at Sofía! Nicolás is the darkest of all. I had fourteen children by him. Only nine are alive; the others are dead.

"When I was young, blacks and whites couldn't marry; it had to be white with white, black with black, *trigueño* [medium dark] with *trigueña.* They say there are only two races, black and white, but the hen gives birth to many chickens. There are *grifos* [very dark], Negroes, *trigueños,* and whites. Sometimes you can't tell a person by his color. For example, someone is perfectly white, and his hair comes out like a black."

Maí Vargas and her husband separated long ago. Now she lives in a comfortable house on the main road with several of her children, one of whom is a wig-maker and hairdresser. Her husband comes often in his big but ancient car to visit the family. They are on good terms and spend the day together quite happily. Señor Vargas is a gentleman of the old school. He has the manners of a Spanish grandee and is extremely polite and gallant toward women. He doesn't understand the modern independent woman with her free ways and aspirations toward a career. The only way to get along with him is to bow to his authority, even though only on small matters. Maí Vargas feeds his vanity by twitting him about the many women in his life. Paí [Father] Vargas, now about seventy years old, smiles at the ladies sitting on the porch and winks at the youngest.

Maí remembers how she worked as a domestic after Paí left her.

"I worked for ten years in Santurce in rich people's houses. Even if I didn't want to work or didn't need the money, it is still necessary to work. Those rich people loved me and pulled me away from my own home. They gave me things. I'd prepare lunch for them and, before leaving at night, the meat and rice. They worked at the Capitol Building.

"Now I have arthritis and I cannot cure it. I was an ironing woman, and I would iron for three days at a time, then wash everything and iron again. I absorbed heat from the iron, and I would get a fever and, because I did this again and again, it never ended. Sometimes I still get attacks of pain—and that is a pain that kills."

Like other Loizans, Maí Vargas has her own version of the origin of the fiesta of Santiago.

According to Maí, "One day, Abelardo, a local fisherman, was sitting under a cork tree in the street in Medianías known as Las

Señor Vargas is a gentleman of the old school.

"Before, we didn't have disorder among young people. Now there is civilization. Disgraceful things are happening."

Carreras when the tide washed a little box up on the shore. It was copper, completely watertight. It had a letter that read, 'He who finds this box must take it to customs in San Juan.' But nobody dared open it. In those days, there were no cars, so the man went to San Juan by boat. The customs man found a statue inside the box and a paper that said, 'My name is Saint James the Apostle, he who won the Spanish Wars.' (Just thinking about it gives me goose pimples!) 'Now, Christian people, I want a festival to be celebrated in my name, processions every day for three days.'

"The elders of the village signed a paper promising to have a fiesta every year. So far, there have been ninety fiestas. That's the way it happened.

"The statue in the box was the *little* Saint James. On the paper was also written, 'I am Saint James of the Children.' Amalio Cruz, a rich man on whose land the saint was found, then said, 'If this statue is for the children, then I will send to Spain for a Saint James of the Men.' I think it cost him about a hundred pesos. Then a woman called Difumera said, 'Now I'm going to buy one for the women,' and that lady collected money for a Saint James of the Women. That's why there are three saints.

"When I was young, twelve people made the fiesta each year. They collected money and made sweets of all kinds. There were coconut and pineapple candy, guava and sweet potato pastes, yucca sweets—barrels and barrels of them. It took months to make and pack them. The dancers would tie their candies in big handkerchiefs and eat while they danced.

"They used oxcarts in the processions. There were no automobiles then. And they hung baskets of coconuts to the sides of cows and calves. The people on top carried banners. The carts were adorned with curtains, branches, and flowers. Holy Mary, that was really pretty! We girls wore a new dress for each of the three processions. That was a luxury!"

There were many ways to have good times when Castor Ayala and Maí Vargas were young. Maí remembers particularly the serenades to celebrate a birthday or an engagement. Musicians played guitars, *güiros* [notched gourds], and *maracas* late at night under their friends' windows.

"The beautiful songs they sang—that was glory!" she recalls. "Everyone prepared sweets for the musicians. The family went to bed but would stay awake for the serenade.

"When a child is born here, everyone cries for him. They bring presents, and they cry because nobody knows the destiny of that child, how his death will be. But, when a child dies, we hold a *baquiné* [wake] and sing songs and play the drums."

Señor Ayala also remembers parties when he was young.

"Every Sunday, there was dancing in different homes or in the dance hall. Older people danced the *danza,* the waltz, *rigaudon,* and the *seguidilla.* But the young had their own dances. They did not mix.

"I remember that most dances finished with a fight. Sometimes they would wreck the dance hall. Generally the fight started when one boy tried to take another's partner.

"There was also cockfighting under the pine groves. They grow the cocks specially for the big Fiesta de los Gallos [Festival of the Cocks] in February. Today, we still have cockfighting but it is not so nice. It is prohibited by law outside of the *gallera* [cockpit].

"What with the *bomba,* dances every Saturday and Sunday, and the cockfighting, here in Loíza the weekends were busy!"

Maí Vargas has mixed feelings about modern life.

"It's O.K. I like it because people's minds are open and everyone is civilized. But, before, we didn't have disorder among young people. It was a saintly and honest life, a Catholic life. Now there is civilization. Disgraceful things are happening. People fight with clubs, sticks, and knives, wounding and killing each other. They are so stupid. And then there are drugs that outsiders bring in. Sometimes detectives catch them, and I feel sorry for them. Poor things!

"I don't mind it, but most people detest it. I am content with what God has given me. I pray for the whole world, for world peace, for my sons and daughters."

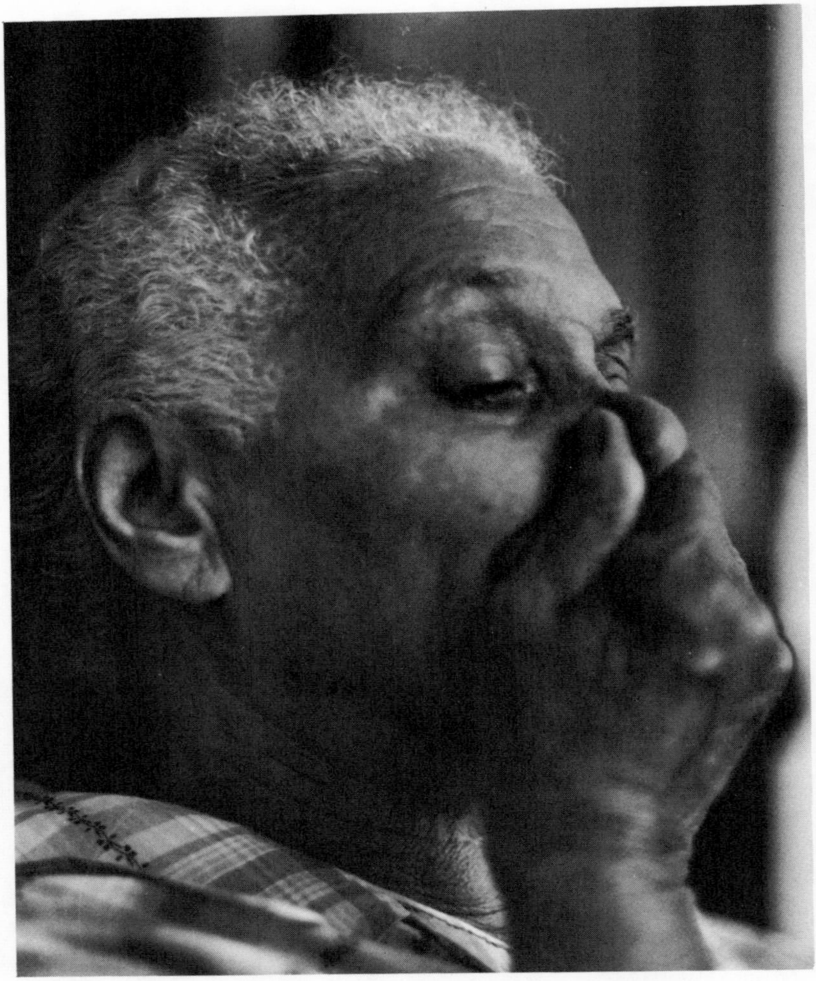

"I pray for the whole world, for world peace, for my sons and daughters."

SOFÍA*

Sofía, Maí Vargas' oldest daughter, is a widow with six children. Her stucco house, poor by American standards, is one of the better ones in Medianías. It has six modestly furnished rooms.

Attractive, tall, and independent, Sofía lives her life openly and fearlessly. Dreams, omens, and visions are as real to her as outward events.

Sofía believes herself to have the special powers of a *bruja* [witch]. She laughed as she began her story:

"I was born during the hurricane of San Cipriano. My mother said it was the worst we ever had and that's why I'm so terrible! My mother's poor wooden shack fell over, and she ran to a rich lady's house. My bellybutton got wet, spoiled, and took a long time to heal. In those days, they cured the bellybutton by burning chicken feathers and smearing it with the ashes. Luckily I didn't get an infection. The *comadrona* [midwife] was like a doctor's or nurse's assistant, and she came every day to bathe the baby and take the mother for a walk and wash her also. All this she did for 2 or 3 pesos. The *comadronas* never studied medicine but were women of courage.

"When I was young, we were very poor. Before the government built the aqueduct, we had open wells with frogs in them. That water was undrinkable. The children suffered from diarrhea and vomiting. Most of us were feeble with big bellies because of the worms and the water. Those who could afford it had big iron containers for storing rainwater and lived more decently.

"By the time I was born, there was civilization here. Some people already had water from the faucet, but not us! There were doctors, automobiles, roads, and people ate meat. But we still carried cans of water on our heads, just as in my mother's time.

"In my grandfather's time, people who owned land usually gave each child a piece after they married. Families were more united then. When the government bought up these farms, that intimate life changed. The government divided the land, gave *parcelas* [plots] to the poorest people, and helped us with money to build a house, like this one I live in.

"We had no store-bought dolls, so we made them out of plants

* Translated from Spanish.

with long roots. We'd wash them and comb the roots as if it were hair and play house with them.

"We had to help out in the house—sweep, carry the water—and be sure to cover the well! We had no stove, only big stones in a square. Finding firewood was fun. We'd balance big heaps of wood on our heads. Sometimes we'd walk in the fields and the bulls would chase us. We'd drop the wood and run.

"Our mothers used the wood for cooking. Those old pots were always covered with sticky grime that nothing could get off. But the food came out much better! We ate sweet potatoes and yucca, cornmeal griddlecakes, baked beans. Today, kids eat meat and they're skinny! We ate cornmeal and were healthy.

"Fruits and vegetables weren't worth anything in those days. A big sack of oranges cost 10 cents. If you didn't have money, they gave it to you. There was abundance because people used to plant everything, and now—with civilization—nobody plants anything. You have to buy it!

"We helped each other by exchanging produce. We grew tomatoes, beans, and other stuff. I'd send a sack of beans to Doña Enriqueta, and she'd send back a sack of yucca.

"We earned very little, but food was cheap. With 75 cents or 6 *reales* [a Spanish coin worth 12½ cents], my mother bought salt pork, ham, tomato sauce, and rice. With 75 cents today we can't buy anything!

"Men, women, and children worked long hours on the plantations cutting cane, picking weeds, fertilizing the soil. Coconuts were picked and shipped to New York and faraway places. In those days, few men went far away to work. I think my father was the only one who did. I used to sell the workers coffee and *bacalaitos* [codfish fried in butter] to make a little money.

"Women also worked as domestics. Now, nobody wants to serve others, because you earn more in the factory, and some places give you transportation, too.

"We have primary and secondary schools in this area. In the old wooden school of Medianías, housewives taught the girls to cook, and men taught the boys to farm and use tools. The best seeds were always sent to the school. They cultivated the best sweet potatoes and raised rabbits, hens, and hogs. We also learned arithmetic and English. A fine thing, that school. If you didn't learn there, it was because you weren't intelligent!

"I was born during
the hurricane
of San Cipriano.
My mother said . . . that's
why I'm so terrible!"

"I did everything, I was really *presenta* [volunteered for everything]. When the teacher went to a meeting, I'd take over the class. I still meet kids, married already, who remember me from that time. Now I'm studying at high school! All I need is four credits to get my diploma. My children go to school during the day and I during the night!

"We had good times when we were young. Our parents let us go dancing, but if a girl got "lost" from the little *cafetines* [coffee houses] where we held our dances, they'd run after us with sticks. Then there was *real running.*

"Today, people dance in bars to juke-box music, but in those days we had Victrolas. We played each record over and over, and some

"I did everything,
I was really presenta.
When the teacher
went to a meeting,
I'd take over the class."

poor guy had to turn the handle round and round. When boys and girls from other places came to our dances, we loved that. I never liked the local boys then, and now I don't like the men here either. My first husband was from Loíza. My second was from Santurce, and his father was from the Dominican Republic.

"Lots of queer things have happened in my life. When I was in seventh grade, my mother worked in Santurce. I brought up the children, fed them, and took care of the house. During this time, I slept in my mother's room. One night, everyone had gone to bed but I couldn't sleep. I felt frightened and left the kerosene lamp burning on the dresser.

"I heard someone open the front door. An old black woman entered my room. She was very thin, tall, and hunchbacked. As she came towards me, I could see her stiffly starched skirt and long-sleeved jacket. I was frightened.

"The hunchback lady took off all her clothes—kerchief, her starched jacket, her enormous bra, a skirt, and another skirt—and put it all on a chair. Then she climbed into my bed. I was afraid to move or scream because my little brother was sleeping next to me. Suddenly I looked at him and saw that he was dead! There we were, the corpse of my brother, the old lady, and me.

"It was a nightmare. Then she began sticking her fingers in my eyes, my ears, my mouth, everywhere she could until daybreak.

"At 5:00, the old lady got dressed, and the corpse became my brother again, but the nightmare was not yet finished. I saw a tiny dwarf about as big as my finger, sitting on a bench, holding a tiny jar. He plucked my pubic hairs one by one. Every time he plucked a hair, a drop of blood fell, and he gathered it into his tiny jar. After a while he waved good-by, put his little bench under his arm, and disappeared through a crack in the floor.

"By this time, it was 9:00 and I was late for school. Miss Becerri, my teacher, came looking for me. She and my sisters entered my room, shook me, and sat me up in bed, but I was so nervous I couldn't talk. Miss Becerri understood that I had had a nightmare and promised to help me.

"They took me to a spiritualist, who explained exerything. He said that behind our house lived an insane woman who believed that my mother had caused the death of one of her children. That woman had been reading those devil books, harmful books that arouse bad spirits. Since my mother wasn't home, all this happened to me instead of her.

"When my mother came home, I told her the whole story. She told me that the same thing had happened to her in Santurce! That spiritualist knew exactly what had happened!"

This event sparked Sofía's interest in spiritualism. From then on, her life was guided in part by dreams and visions, which helped her to value her own power and insights.

"One day mother said, 'Sofía, clean the backyard.' That night, I dreamed I swept so much sand away that I uncovered a hard surface like concrete. It had a handle. I lifted the handle and saw a path with a stairway. I walked to the bottom of the steps and saw a long table and twelve chairs. I knew it was the table of the Last Supper. Straight ahead, on top of a boulder, Jesus Christ was sitting, holding a long shepherd's crook. I felt such happiness that I stared at him —very respectfully. He said to me, 'I've been waiting for you. I want you to come every day and clean this place, but don't tell anyone, or you will not be able to find the door again.'

"I swept the floor, washed the dishes, and put them away. He sat there happy as could be. Then I said good-by and left.

"The next day I had the same dream. I went back and repeated the same chores. But, on the third day, my heart was so overflowing with happiness that I told my mother the whole story. 'Mama, I feel so good when I'm down there. Outside it's hot and there it is cool. It's so beautiful, so delicious!' And she said, 'Is that true?' And I said, 'Come and see for yourself.'

"We sneaked out of the house so no one would see us. He treated us well and was, as always, so happy. I said, 'This is my mother. You told me not to tell anyone, and I'm not going to tell anyone else, but please let my mother stay.' He didn't answer, only smiled and seemed happy we were both there. The next day I couldn't find the door anymore.

"My first marriage wasn't even a marriage. I was only in my third year of high school. I was ignorant and didn't even know how to put on make-up or when my period was to come!

"I had no help from my parents. My father had abandoned us and my mother had to work in Santurce. I had to take care of the others.

"I had this boyfriend and I liked him very much. Then I committed that error, as we say, *metí la pata* [put my foot in it]. When the school year was over, I was three months pregnant. I didn't notice, but my boyfriend and my neighbors did. I was skinny, and they could see my belly. Then my mother told me about the birds and the bees. 'Well,' she said, 'you will just have to leave home!'

"The boy arranged for me to live with his aunt. I suffered very much, but he helped me. A year after Pipe was born, they married the boy to an old lady. He was eighteen and she was thirty-two. I didn't try to push him into marrying me. Even when you're poor, you have pride!

"I went back to my mother's house. They didn't want me there, because I had done such a foolish thing. I worked hard and tried to make them like me, but my younger sisters pushed me around. Finally, my father let down his grudge. He loved my son, and so did everybody else.

"I was alone for two years. I lived among women and not girls any more. Because I had sinned, I was freer than before. I knew how to take care of myself. I didn't lose faith just because I had a child out of wedlock. I could still be happy because I wanted to be happy! I had lots of men friends—but they were all the same, just like the first one. He came back just before shipping out in the merchant marine and asked me to still care for him. 'I'll never get anything from him,' I thought, 'so I better find my own way.'

"Life was hard. I couldn't continue studying and had no job. I knew I must find a man to take care of me and my son.

"When I met Gómez, I was very skinny, for I had been nursing Pipe for three years! In my mother's house, we ate the leftovers, but that wasn't enough and I had to nurse him.

"I don't know how Gómez fell in love with me, because I looked like a skeleton. But he did, the father of my children, and I trusted him from the first moment. 'I'm going to be your husband,' he said. 'No,' I said, 'I already have one.' I was scared to death. He was a veteran and single and, even though he knew my story, he still wanted to marry me. I liked him because he was ugly but very clean, a neat black guy. I accepted him and proved to him that the woman who is difficult to get is the most valuable.

"My husband was a boxer and a playboy. Even though he was ugly, he had really nice women. I never saw them, but I knew because of lipstick stains and things. I have a terrible temper and would get jealous. We'd fight until we were black and blue. 'Well,' he'd say, 'you think you've got guts, you want to try a few punches with me? Come on!' He'd try not to hit me too hard, but I'd come out with a big shiner. I'd look in the mirror, and seeing that black eye made me even madder. I'd put my fist in the air, spit on it and, as he turned around, I'd knock him out!

"Sometimes we would take a walk afterwards, but neither of us would look at anyone—both of us with shiners, he in the left and I in the right! Two blackouts and no grudges. You hit me and I hit you. We're even. Then he would say, 'Let's go eat at *Luquillo* or *Las Croabas.*'

"Everybody marveled at my husband. He was so strong and active, a good car salesman. A week before he died, we were sitting on the porch planning changes in the house. Suddenly my mind seemed to float away. I saw a luxurious coffin, like for a President, with an American flag on it. I screamed and hid my face in his lap. 'What's the matter?' he asked, and I told him what I saw.

"But I did the wrong thing. Instead of crying that time, I should have called upon Jesus Christ to give me strength to fight back. I should have sprinkled holy water around the room, and the spirit would have gone away. But I was yellow that night and did nothing.

"I don't say Gómez died because someone did anything to him. He died because God wanted him up there. Here on earth, you can only kill with a gun or a knife. If my throat hurts or my foot is sprained, it's not because someone is sticking pins in me. It's part of your organism to get sick . . . you understand.

"One night around 1:30, I heard Daisy, who slept by Gómez' side, say, 'Mommy!' I didn't really awaken. 'Mommy,' she said, 'don't you hear?' 'Daisy, go to sleep; it's the dog,' I said and rolled over on my side. 'Mommy, don't you hear, it's Poppy.' I jumped out of bed and turned the lights on. It was true—my husband was in agony. His face was disfigured and part of his body cold.

"My little sons, Papirito and Rolando, screamed, 'Poppy is dead, Poppy is dead.' I shouted that he was only suffocated.

"I bent over him to hear his breath. Perhaps I did him wrong, but he died right there.

"Without thinking, I got back into bed with him. By this time, the house was full of people shouting for me to get out of bed.

"Then the police came. 'He's dead,' they said, but I didn't understand them. They wrapped him in canvas and, even then, I couldn't believe he was dead. In the morning, an ambulance took him away.

"I didn't lose faith just because I had a child out of wedlock."

"When Gómez died, Daisy and I were badly affected. She adored him and couldn't forget he died at her side.

"But Alberto held it all back. After three months, he complained that his heart was constantly moving around. It was so swollen anyone could see it. That fever made him crazy like a madman. He also said that flowers and other objects were talking and singing to him. The doctor said there was nothing wrong, but he just lay in bed and didn't eat a thing. Then I put him in the hospital. He was there for a whole month, but the medicines the doctors gave him didn't do him any good.

"Then I took him to a spiritualist. I would try anything to cure him. The first time, I went alone. The lady didn't know me and I didn't know her, not even her name. She said, 'You have a boy in the hospital; take him out. There is nothing wrong with him; only his father wants him to die. So the same heart suffocation your husband died of is reflected in your son. The doctors understand nothing.'

"In a gallon bottle she poured waters of different colors. 'Bathe him with this,' she said, 'and he will recuperate. But, in three months, he will show signs again. Then come back.' I did what she told me to do, and with faith. The illness disappeared.

"When the doctor saw him again, he asked me how he got well, and I said, 'Just by resting.' I didn't dare tell him what had happened. 'Ay, Virgin!' he said, 'that boy looks so healthy!'

"After three months, Alberto fell into it again. This time, Alberto went with me to the lady. She gave him the same waters and prayed over him. She said that she removed Alberto from his father's power. He's been fine ever since, and that was a year and a half ago!"

Many Puerto Ricans believe in spiritualism. Loíza, on the North Coast, and the lovely town of Guayama, on the South Coast, have long been famous for their mediums.

Sofía says, "I have all the spiritual development I need to be a medium. Other people have more knowledge, but I'm a clairvoyant. I see things simply by talking to people.

"Spiritualism isn't a real paid profession. People give spiritualists a peso or half a peso—whatever they can afford. You can't live on that! But I don't charge for services, because to me it's a charity. God gave me this gift to help others, and you can't charge for that. If someone gives me a doughnut or a cake, I'll appreciate it, but money, no. A charity is a charity."

"Yes, one has to doubt, but one has to believe also."

For Sofía, the forces of good and evil are always present. When she feels spirits in the house, she exorcises them by yelling, praying, and sprinkling the room with holy water.

"I pray to God to keep me from evil. I want to belong to God, not Satan. In my dreams, I cure crippled and sick men just by putting my hand on them. I would cure thousands of people, not with medicines but with plants that other people don't know about. They are everywhere, and I have cured with them.

"Some dreams scare me, but they are demonstrations of my powers. For instance, I didn't know you [this writer] were coming here today but, two days ago, I dreamed I saw you right where you're sitting now!"

One afternoon, Sofía and her brother Nicolás sat on the shady porch of her house and talked about religion. She said, "We are Catholics but spiritualism is also Catholic because it is based on God. Every prayer mentions God. Every prayer begins with 'In the name of the Father, the Son, and the Holy Ghost, amen.' We have different prayers for each problem. If you need money, the spiritualist will say 'Your husband doesn't earn enough, and the money you have goes through your fingers like *sal y agua* [salt and water]. You take a bath to tone up your luck. Mix mint leaves and honey, a bit of brown sugar, and boil it. Let it cool, then rub it on. Now pray to 'the Good Luck' and forget about it. The money won't come immediately, but soon you'll get a job or income from somewhere.

"But suppose it doesn't work. What can you lose, and what harm can it do you?

"When I feel sick, I go to the doctor. If he can't help me, I go to a spiritualist. I'm not going to let myself die just like that. *God has given these people understanding.* Yes, one has to *doubt,* but one has to *believe* also."

One of the most thriving businesses in Puerto Rico (and in New York) is the *botánica.* These little shops are found everywhere, in shopping centers, in market places, and along the streets of every city and town. They sell prayer books, recorded prayers, magazines, pictures and statues of saints, medicines, dried herbs, and plants. Most medicines are specially prepared, but some, like homeopathic pills and powders, are known to the medical profession. The variety of prayers is enormous. Sofía's *Collection of Spiritual Prayers,* subtitled *Message from the Infinite,* contains prayers for San Silvestre, Saint Joan (of Arc), and Saint Malta. There are prayers for special spiritual forces—the Just Judge, guardian angels, the Holy Shirt, and an Indian prayer. Among the most powerful are the African Powers, each with its own color—Alegua (black), Alofi (red), Orula (green), Ocun (white), Shango (brown), Obacala (blue), Ochum (yellow), and Yemala (red).

Each saint or power has a special mission. The Holy Shirt protects against bodily harm. "There are people," says Sofía, "who have been shot at but not killed because the bullet hit a button or a belt buckle. Then there was a man arrested for carrying a gun and disrupting the peace. He could have got four or five years in jail, but with the prayer to the Just Judge—nothing!"

One day, a woman Sofía knew threatened her with a knife. Sofía defended herself with a machete. The case came up before the judge.

"Madam," he said to Sofía, "you may leave. You are a decent woman—but I fine this other lady $100."

"That day I used a prayer that said, 'With two I see you, with three I tie you, your blood I will drink, and your heart will break.' That's why nothing happened to me!

"We believe each person is born with his own guardian angel. When you're born, God sends that angel to guard and protect you from evil. When the person dies, the angel disappears."

Sofía's mother, Maí Vargas, has her own view of spiritualism:

"Once, long ago, someone found secret scriptures hidden in the church. They stole those books and let their relatives read them. That's how spiritualism spread. I never wanted to take that religion into my soul, because I'm convinced it has something to do with Satan. Sofía doesn't believe that, but *I who am older do believe it*!"

Sofía's views on women's independence vary with the situation:

"I never worked outside when I was married. My husband used to say work was for men. He believed that Puerto Rican women were modest, that contact with the city would spoil them, make them pick up bad habits like smoking, drinking, and wearing vulgar clothes.

"Women here are humble as long as their men support them. May God pardon me for what I'm saying, but that's the truth. I am as frank as I am ugly, but Puerto Rican women who work think they're big bosses and try to run their husbands. That's why there are so many divorces and separations!"

Whatever her opinions of the aggressive modern woman, Sofía herself is no clinging vine. "Now, I'll tell you the truth, it's not that I like to boss people around, but I want to be respected. I want people to give a damn when I talk. People say I'm tough. Well, if they mean I won't put up with abuse, they're right. My husband never harassed me, because he knew I'd harass him back. I'm a woman of temperament.

"But, if my husband needs help, I'll wear pants and work like a man. If my man can't feed us for some reason, I'll work for both of us—and with all my heart, and I'm happy.

"The people here are terrible gossips. They want to know what you have and don't have, what you've done and haven't done—past, present, and future. I stand up to them. I don't deny or hide anything about my life. Nothing they say can hurt or bother me. Anyway, I'm a free woman and do what I like.

"Not long ago, some kid broke my little nephew's arm. When I heard about it, I got tough. When I get mad, it's like starting a car mmmMMMM! . . . and I can kill someone! So I go and I call Julia, the kid's mother. Nobody answered. Seven times I called her, and finally she came out with the kid grabbing her skirt—a huge kid. 'Tell your kid,' I scream, 'if he ever does anything to my kids, I'll kill him!'

"About a week later, just as I was going to bed, I hear my gate open. I open the door to the living room, and I see Julia's husband [Guillermo] sitting on a chair drunk and mooing like a cow. And I said, 'Pipe down! If you want to see me, you'd better behave, but, if you shout, I'll kick you out.'

"The shouting continued. Finally I grabbed Guillermo by the arm and shoved him out of the house. 'I wish you were a man,' he hollered. 'I am, in my own way,' I shouted back. 'If you try anything, I'll rip your heart out!' 'Daisy,' I said to my daughter, 'bring me the butcher knife.'

"I picked up Guillermo's bike and swung it over the fence. It crashed to the ground. He threatened me: 'I'll bring your mother here and she'll shame you!' I chased him down the street.

"Later on, I heard what happened at my mother's house. 'Oh Señora,' Guillermo cried, 'that girl of yours is crazy! This bike is not mine and she broke it, and she said she'd take *you* by the legs and smack me dead with you!' My brother said, 'Go in peace. I'll teach that sister of mine a lesson.'

"But they never came. Nobody gives orders here but me, not even Papa or Mama, nor that man that is with me, nor my kids, nor anyone."

Since her husband's death, Sofía has been trying to finish her high school education. She also talks about taking special courses to qualify her for skilled jobs. "I like men's work, but I don't want to be a janitor or a school cook, because mopping floors and cooking I can do in my own house, but I might like to be a dietician. To be a janitor is to be nothing. I've wanted to be a judge because you'd know the truth and who's guilty and put order in things. But there are no women judges here!"

Sofía has had a number of lovers since her husband died, but she is no lady of easy virtue. "I have boyfriends, but I live alone. A man has to court me for at least a month for me to see if he's really going to benefit me. I don't go just for pleasure; I have to respect a man too—he has to be a somebody. There is nothing as beautiful as having the right kind of man 'represent' you. When you're alone, men come around, but I don't have the temperament for that kind of life. That's why I study them and give them a chance to study me. Sometimes I am convenient for them and they for me.

"The first man I had died and the second too, but I can't just cry about the past. The man I have now is really helpful. Sometimes I come home and find the house clean, the floors mopped, and the rice and beans cooked. He takes care of my kids and never talks rough to them. He can give advice but, if he comes with a lot of 'Ah AHAHAH, AH' I'd tell him, 'Beat it! Is this *your* house?'

"A man has to come humbly. You have something? Share it with me. I have something too; here—have some. But he can't be my boss. I don't want big gifts either. Food, clothing, shoes, money—I'll take those any time. Big gifts—when I can afford them. I live as God wants me to. I don't want any more than I deserve!"

For almost two years after her husband's death, Sofía's life was filled with trouble. She was constantly distressed by lack of money and purpose. The worst of that period was the suicide of a man she was genuinely fond of and the premature marriage of her sixteen-year-old son. During this time she had violent seizures that left her exhausted but momentarily relieved. Life improved when a new man appeared.

"My boyfriend is a very nice man. He has a family, and his wife seems to like me, but she has a terrible temper. She doesn't know her husband is with me. One day, I went to the *espiritista,* and she told me, 'A lady you do not know is coming to see you.' The next day I look out the window and see a lady sitting on the porch. I know right away it was her. My boyfriend hid in the house. 'Come in,' I said politely, and I ask her what her business is. 'People tell me my husband is in your house,' she says in a loud voice. 'Oh no,' I say, 'I have many friends, but I don't think I know him. What's his name?' And she tells me. 'I never heard of him,' I said, 'maybe you are mixing me up with someone else. Listen, do I look like the kind of person who would do such a thing. I have six children and I am a widow.' By this time, I see that she is not so angry. 'If you want to look in my house,' I say, 'you are welcome. I have nothing to hide.'

" 'No,' she says, 'I cannot do that. The people who told me about you must be mistaken.' Finally she went away. You see, if I had admitted anything, everybody would have been unhappy. She would fight with her husband; he would be nervous and worried and she would follow him; and I would be unhappy too. This way I reassure her and everybody is happy. . . . Anyway, I don't want marriage—I don't trust men.

"About my boyfriend—I didn't fall for him; he fell for me. He doesn't demand anything of me, and he has no evil in him. He's simple and considerate. He's a somebody, and I like people who are somebodies, even if we have nothing to eat but dough.

"My boyfriend works in Río Piedras but lives in Loíza with his family. I'm sure they lack for nothing. The salary from his job goes to his wife—and the extra money he earns, to me. I say, 'Divide it—half for your wife and half for me.' You understand, I'm not a hypocrite. I don't need his salary, because I feed my children from their father's pension. Of course, I don't tell him that. He has to take care of me because I don't need a man just for decoration!

"I can't live alone, and I'm proud of what I am. The man who's with me never lacks affection. That's why it's easy to love me and hard to leave me. God may punish me, but I think he won't find reason for it. One of the Commandments says you shouldn't covet your neighbor's man, but it's not my fault that men fall in love with me!"

SONGS

The word *aguinaldo* means a Christmas present and also a Christmas song. Brought from Spain in Colonial times, *aguinaldos* are sung in the mountains and along the coast to this very day. Every night during the holiday season, singers go caroling from house to house. In return, they receive rum, barbecued pig, or delicious meat-filled pastries—or affection. Of course, no payment might provoke a rebuke, as the words of the song below imply. This *aguinaldo* was sung by Sofía Vargas and her sister Ana Iris. Their children played the accompaniment on percussion "instruments" found around the house—bashed-in beer cans and empty tomato cans.

Ábreme la puerta *que yo quiero entrar;* *he hecho mis pasteles* *no quieren quedar.*	Open the door for me, For I want to enter. I have made my little pastries. They are not to be wasted.
Chorus *A la salendera, a la salendera;* *a la salendera de mi corazón.*	 To the joy, to the joy; To the joy of my heart.

But what we want is
Affection and kindness.

Ay, adentro veo	Oh, I see inside,
en mucho tapado;	Covered all over.
no se si será	I don't know if it will be
un lechón asado.	a roasted pig.
Si no tiene nada	If you have nothing,
nada nos dará;	Nothing will you give us,
pero lo que queremos	But what we want is
cariño y bondad.	Affection and kindness.
Óigame, Enriqueta.	Listen to me, Henrietta.
la quiero y la adoro;	I love you and adore you,
pero mi aguinaldo	But my *aguinaldo*
no se lo perdono.	I do not forgive you.
Vengo del olivo.	I come from the olive tree.
voy para el olivar.	I go to the olive grove.
un año que viene	As one year comes,
otro que se va.	The other one goes.
Esta casa tiene	This house has
la cuesta de acero;	A steel slide;
los que viven dentro	Those who live inside
son los caballeros.	Are gentlemen.

Buenas noches. Goodnight.

Here is a popular *plena* that advises women how to deal with their men according to appropriate spiritualistic practice:

Cuando las mujeres	When the women
quieren a los hombres,	Love their men,
prenden cuatro velas,	They light four candles
y se las ponen por los rincónes.	And set them in the corners.
Compran esos libros	They buy those books
que se llaman de colecciónes;	That are called collections;
van a la cocina,	They go to the kitchen
y le hacen sus oraciónes.	And say their prayers.
Rompen la camisa, los calzon-cillos,	They tear the shirt, the socks,

los pantalones;	The trousers—
pobre de los hombres,	Those poor men!
las comidas se las componen.	The dinners they throw together!
Y le echan huesos de muerto	And they throw bones of death;
agua florida tambíen le ponen,	Scented water they also use.
ay madre querida	Oh, mother—beloved,
ten cuidado con ésos hombres.	Take care with those men!
Si son de Guayama	If they're from Guayama,
hechizos ellas le ponen,	They cast spells on them
en un vaso de agua,	In a glass of water.
todo el cuerpo le descomponen.	The whole body they dissolve.

Using the tune of the same *plena,* students protesting the war in Vietnam wrote a new verse:

Cuando las mujeres	When the women
quieren a los hombres,	Love their men,
ellas no permiten	They do not permit
que se los lleven los invasores.	The invaders to carry them off.

RAÚL AYALA

We have seen Loíza through the eyes of some of its older inhabitants. However, even the young people are very attached to their village and folkways despite encroaching modernization.

Raúl Ayala, son of Castor, says, "I was born here, and I like this town. When I build a house, it will be here. But, if 'progress' kills off our tradition, I won't want to live here any more. Years ago, they used to have *bomba* in Santurce. Then outsiders moved in and complained to the police about the noise. Now nobody plays any more. I don't care if they make twenty thousand buildings here, just as long as we keep our festival."

Raúl, a university student, challenged many old village values. To the question "Who will rule the household when you marry?" his first response was "I will," then he shook his head. "Oh, no, both of us will; she has the same rights I have! The age of male privilege has passed. I believe in democracy. Nothing good is accomplished by force."

"When I build a house it will be here."

Raúl is a diligent student, but he admits that he cannot concentrate—something that never happened to him before. The English textbooks, the English-speaking teacher, her culture and experience are totally foreign to him. There is little communication between teacher and student.

THE LOCAL PRIEST

Another view of life in the area is expressed by the priest, a young man recently arrived in Loíza, who has mixed feelings about his parishioners. "More women work here than men; the men just sit around in bars or on street corners. As long as they earn a couple of pennies a day, they're happy. After that's spent, they go back to work, not before. Women and rum! That's all they care about.

"In Canóvanas [seat of the municipality of Loíza], the people are more responsible. They all work every day and live with dignity.

"My mission here is to help these people amount to something. They should have cooperatives, social organizations, and more factories.

"In Puerto Rico, *thanks to God and the Americans,* there's so much work, and I cannot understand why there's so much poverty—unless it is the people's own fault.

"But they are very nice. They treat each other equally, regardless of color. Sometimes the little children argue about who is lighter than the other, and I scold them for this. But adults have no prejudice. Even their spiritualism is harmless. I'm afraid the early missionaries overemphasized the veneration of the saints. Now, people think they can get anything by burning candles in front of their favorite saints. But those spiritualists are nice people. I go among the people with high hopes, but they think I'm not sincere."

POVERTY: COLOBÓ, SAN ISIDRO

Poverty is seen everywhere in Medianías. A two-minute walk from the main road leads one to areas of broken-down, unpainted shacks. Nothing in Medianías, however, compares with conditions in the nearby barrio Colobó [an Indian word meaning Negro community]. From a distance, Colobó is beautiful. It is situated near the beach among huge palms and lush fruit trees. Up close, the debris, the dilapidated shacks, and the stench of outhouses offend the senses.

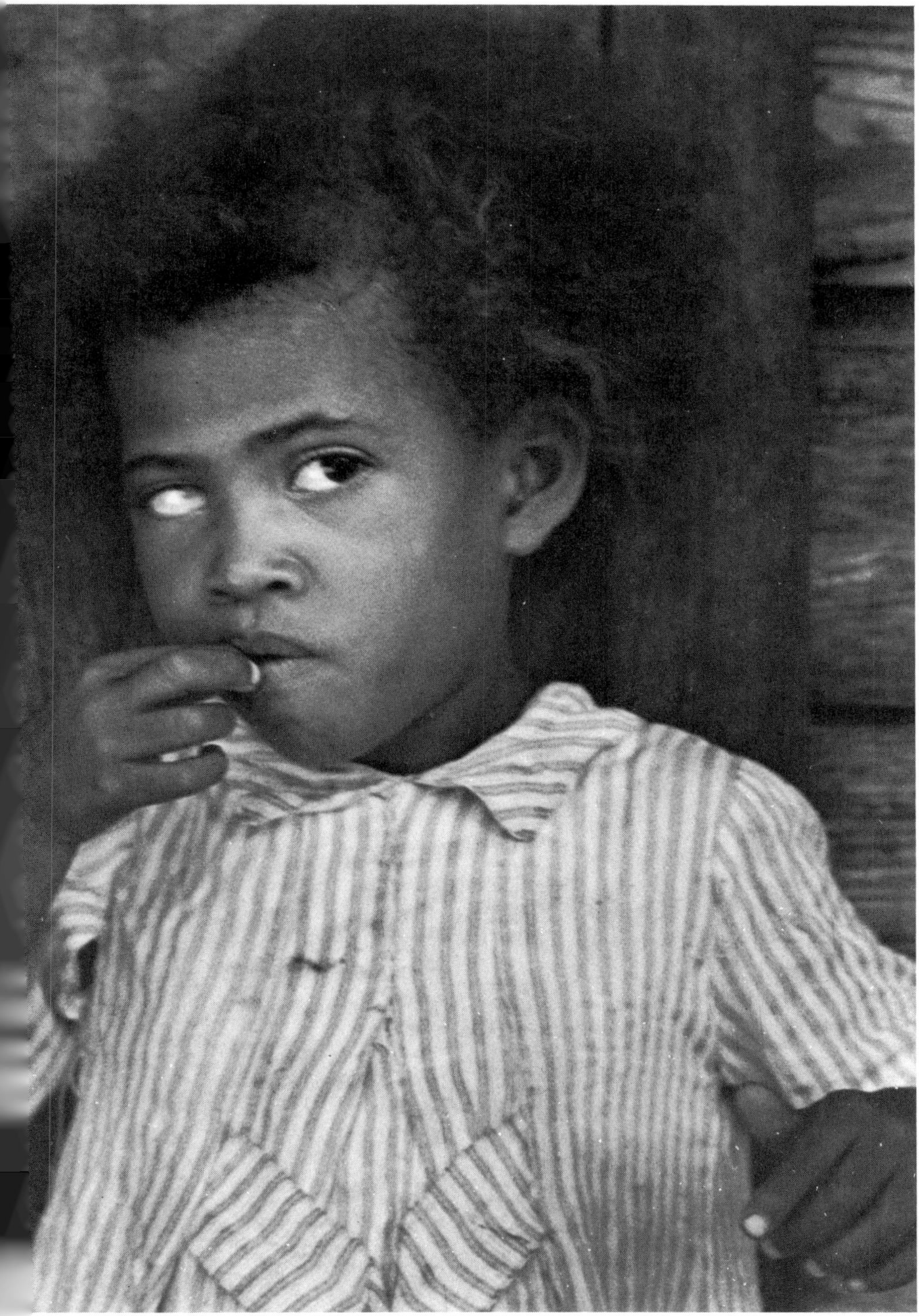

Few houses have electricity or running water. Many wells are contaminated.

The public health officer of nearby Carolina occasionally inspects the area. "Things have somewhat improved here," he says. "Many concrete houses are being built, a few with running water. A few years ago, you wouldn't have eaten in most of these huts, they were so dirty.

"But such improvements are only a drop in the bucket. Children suffer from malnutrition, parasites, and anemia. We help these children, give them blood transfusions, and generally improve their health, then we send them back to the same environment. Six months later, they are back in the hospital for treatment!

"In Carolina, we have a team of social workers, nurses, health educators, and doctors working on community problems. In Loíza, people get only minimal medical attention. That's not enough!

"They need to be educated about diet. Crabs and fresh fish are plentiful here and good for children. But many people believe children cannot digest such food, so they give it to the old folks.

"The Loízans are supposed to use the Canóvanas hospital, but they come to us because we're near the U.S. Marines area and have better facilities. Seventeen of the twenty beds in my pediatric ward are now occupied by children from Loíza. If someone needs medical service, I give it, no matter where the patient comes from.

"Obviously we need more personnel. Washington could help, if it wanted to, by granting our doctors the same options as U.S. doctors—the choice of two years in public health services or the armed forces. Because of our political situation, it is very difficult to get federal action on any issue. On the local level, yes, but from Washington, doubtful."

Traditionally, social change in Spanish-speaking countries is effected by political bargaining rather than by citizens' action. However, direct social action is on the increase. In 1969, a group of impoverished families of the San Isidro barrio of Loíza took over unused government property and began construction of houses. This action stirred up a hornets' nest and has yet to be resolved in the courts.

The people of the barrio have been aided by the U.S.-funded Legal Services, Inc. According to one of its lawyers, "The barrio is extremely poor and overcrowded. The majority have no regular work, and several families live together in small houses. Ten or

"The people took things into their own hands and started to build."

twelve people live in a single room with four or five to a bed.

"During the election campaign a year ago, politicians running for office promised them *parcelas* [plots of land] for new construction. Since then, the people have petitioned the government many times, but absolutely nothing has been done—nothing.

"So the people took things in their own hands and started to build on the government-owned meadowland surrounding San Isidro. Most of the land is unused. The police came and arrested about 125 people, but the judge ruled that the squatters were within their rights to build on unused government property.

"So the people went back home, happy with the legal decision. The police promised to go away, but they stayed on, and soon began to intimidate the people by writing their names down and warning them to stop building."

Interviewed at the building site, the police said that the squatters' action was illegal, and that the trouble was caused by outsiders. "The people of this barrio are fine citizens when we are alone with them. But, as soon as somebody else talks to them, they get loud. But we don't listen. We protect property, but we don't use violence, arrest anybody, or do anything illegal!"

Aroused by the police threats, the people decided to demonstrate at the governor's residence in San Juan.

Truckloads of people singing and carrying picket signs left for San Juan, chanting:

"*Parcelas, sí!*" ("Land, yes!")
"*Desahuicios, no!*" ("Evictions, no!")

Although in high spirits, the villagers really feared a confrontation with the police. The demonstrators were received politely at the governor's palace and were assured that the case would be resolved in their favor. Back in the barrio, they held a victory celebration.

Two days later, the government obtained a court order enjoining the squatters from further construction. The people were accused of destroying grazing land, but were able to prove this was false. However, the crucial question of squatters' rights was not yet resolved.

This parody on a traditional song sung at a *baquiné,* [wake] was sung by the San Isidro squatters:

Por el alma de Ferré	For the soul of Ferré [the name of the governor]
vamos todos a rogar.	Let us all pray.
que Dios lo saque de penas	May God remove his sorrows
y lo lleve a un sitio "nice."	And take him to a *nice* place.

The Legal Service lawyers told of social action that has occurred elsewhere on the Island. "In Ponce [Puerto Rico's second largest

Parcelas,
sí!
Desahuicios,
no!

Land,
yes!
Evictions,
no!

city], the court ordered two hundred families to vacate an area belonging to millionaire landowners. These people have been living there for a long time. Unless something is done, the houses will be destroyed and they will be thrown out. The people are fighting for their homes, and we defend them in court.

"A government-owned corporation called Corporation for Urban Renewal and Living sells land and apartments in housing developments at supposedly reasonable prices. But these people only get part-time jobs. Last year, the people protested the high cost of the land. The police shot at them, injuring many. You can still see the bullet holes in the houses!"

Legal Services, Inc., was set up in 1967 by the Office of Economic Opportunities in Washington to provide legal aid for poor people. A basic task is to make people conscious of their rights as citizens. "We have been called Communists and anarchists by local politicians, but they haven't been able to do anything against us. We are not sure how Washington feels about us but, when one official was informed of our activities, he said, 'If the Puerto Rican government is attacking Legal Services, you must be doing something good!'

"The official rate of unemployment is 9 per cent, but that doesn't include part-time workers. The income of many people here doesn't come to more than $600 a year. They are agricultural workers and part-time factory workers. If the factory is slow or closes, they are thrown out first. The unions are not strong enough to help them."

5
Mita

For hundreds of years, the Catholic church controlled religious life in Puerto Rico as in other Spanish-speaking countries. When the Americans took over in 1898, several Protestant denominations established missions on the Island and trained Puerto Ricans as ministers. These churches are still largely American-supported. Later on, Jehovah's Witnesses and Pentecostal congregations became popular, particularly among the poor.

The only native Puerto Rican church, however, is the cult of Mita. Established in 1940, it claims a membership of more than ten thousand. Its principal temple is in the Hato Rey section of San Juan, but there are others in Puerto Rico, the United States, and the Dominican Republic.

Juanita García Peraza, or Mita, as she is called by her followers, was born of wealthy parents in Hatillo and raised in Arecibo. At her death on February 21, 1970, she was seventy-two years old. Although she disclaimed divinity, she firmly believed that God had chosen her to do his work. "I was very sick once," she said. "A Catholic sister said to me, 'Why don't you pray directly to God?' I promised the Lord that, if he would heal me, I would leave everything and preach. The Lord healed me, and I have been serving Him ever since. When Jesus Christ died, He said, 'I will send the Holy Spirit; I will send a Comforter.' It's the Spirit of God who gives me the prophecies. It's *Papa* [God] who is here."

Mita's followers believe she is the voice of God, the Prophet of the twentieth century, as Moses and Jesus were of their times.

"You feel a joy you can't explain."

"Her mystery," says one of Mita's ministers, "is the mystery of love. She calls all to salvation—rich and poor, black and white."

A follower explained, "God is a voice, a Spirit who manifests Himself in human beings when He pleases. First He came as the Father, Jehovah—then as Jesus, the Son—and now as Mita, the Mother. Each had His time and His work to do for the Lord. But, today, the sons of God still don't want to obey His orders. That's why God sent Mita to us. Through Mita, you will hear the voice of God. After the service is over, if you believe, you raise your right hand, and then the Holy Spirit starts working on you. Then you meet God. All the persons in the temple of Mita have met God Himself, the Spirit."

"It's the Spirit of God who gives me the prophecies."

To help the needy, the church operates a nonprofit cooperative. All members can buy shares. The cooperative owns property near the temple—groceries, bakeries, restaurants, hardware and furniture stores. On her *finca* [estate] near Arecibo, on Puerto Rico's North Shore, Mita raised crops and kept animals and birds. The enormous house served as a hostel for her followers when they came for consultations.

Mita's relationship to her congregation was personal. One of her administrators said, "Every morning seventy or eighty of our brothers come to her house. Mita gives each one a dollar. If someone can't pay the rent, we pay it. We help anyone who can't help himself. We never ask for money during our services. If people want to give, they can. Nothing is compulsory. All our money comes from our business enterprises." Mita was famous for her healing. Hundreds of people have reported cures.

The congregation of Mita is ultraconservative. Its moral tone is more forbidding than that of the older Christian churches. "Before I met Mita," says one of her administrators, "my life was pleasures and vices—women, dancing, gambling, drinking. My whole family suffered for my sins. But, when I met Mita, fear entered my heart. Instead of a party, I'd go to church and pray. I began to receive love from my brothers there, and I gave love. I am happy. Those illnesses caused by sin have disappeared."

The counselors of the church talk to the children about the evil in the world. "We tell them they must obey their parents and love God. In that way, they grow up doing good to the church, the community, and the whole world. They are examples of goodness—they don't dance, don't smoke, don't gamble, don't drink. They are dedicated to their church."

Cut off from dances and parties, Mita's young followers make up for it by singing and clapping during the four weekly services. Afterward, small, animated groups gather in the street to sing and play guitars. The balmy night air resounds with the ecstatic religious words set to popular tunes.

The temple of Mita in Hato Rey is a large square room seating about two thousand. On the clean white walls are inscriptions from the Bible, written in large blue letters. On one side is the platform for Mita and her administrators. Bandstands on the other three are reserved for two large brass bands and a string ensemble.

The hall is noisy and crowded with men, women, and children

"They came from all over Puerto Rico."

dressed in white from head to foot. The impassioned preachers easily arouse the crowd. As the singing begins, the people rise to their feet. The voices, the clapping, and the stamping become louder and louder; bodies sway from side to side to the rhythm. Shouts of joy well up from the crowd, almost drowning out the song. The fervor mounts, and as the song reaches its climax, a roar sweeps the hall. Then—complete silence.

The high point was always Mita's own appearance. Preceded by a blaring brass band, she would walk down the main aisle of the temple—a bright, joyous figure, smiling and waving a white handkerchief. On its feet and mad with joy, the crowd would sing and shout, waving handkerchiefs in return.

Even nonbelievers sensed Mita's capacity for love, which was probably the secret of her success. She loved people, and all other living things—birds, animals—the earth itself. On her *finca,* she kept birds, cows, sheep, dogs, and horses; in the garden of the Hato Rey temple, flamingos and other beautiful creatures of unusual plumage and color.

Mita's temple in New York is located on Manhattan's West Side. Although it is smaller than the parent temple, its members are no less devoted. Until Mita's death, her New York followers frequently made pilgrimages to Puerto Rico. Because they hoped ultimately to return to the Island, they had no cooperatives in New York. Shortly before she died, Mita appointed twelve disciples, who claim to receive and transmit God's messages. The church is continuing its work.

"We like New York," said Carmen, a twenty-year-old member of Mita's New York congregation, "and God has placed us here for a purpose: to tell the American people about Mita's work. We try to make friends with them. It's a sacrifice being here, but we enjoy it.

"I used to go to Catholic and Pentecostal services, but the only time I felt happy was when I joined this church. We do what the Holy Spirit tells us to do, and what's in our hearts. If we do the right thing, then God is always with us.

"I walk out on the street day or night without being afraid. Nothing happens to me, because I know He is going to protect me. That's why I feel happy and safe all the time.

"I joined the church two years ago and, ever since, it's been happiness and glory all the way. You feel a joy you can't explain, because it's so great. You can't look it up in the dictionary—there are no words!"

In the front of the church, there are three lights—red, white, and

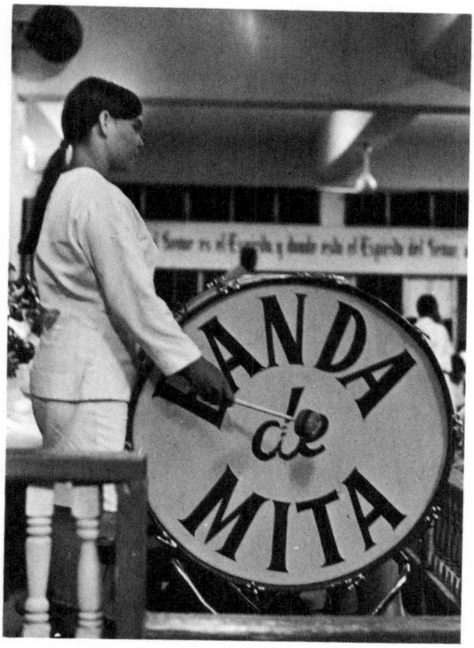

"They are dedicated to their church."

blue—which stand for love, liberty, and unity. "When this church was founded," said the minister, "we were told by revelation to preach these three messages because people are lacking in religion these days. We need love—love between members, unity of all people in one church, and freedom. We must be free of sin and all the chains that hold us down, like *machismo* [male domination]."

In Puerto Rico, the cult of Mita is accorded respect by government and press. As a potential political force it is not to be antagonized or ignored. Mita's funeral, in February, 1970, was noted in the San Juan *Star:* "They came from all over Puerto Rico . . . and from New York, Philadelphia, and Kansas, to pay their last respects to the dead religious leader. The mourners easily filled the 2,300-seat temple in Hato Rey. They flowed out into the street and silently watched their fellow mourners file past the bier.

"One church member said, 'A lot of people think the properties belong to Mita, but they belong to the church or the cooperative. A 15 to 20 percent annual dividend goes to its members.' An onlooker commented, 'This is the first church I've seen that doesn't milk the people!'

"An honor guard stood around the coffin, drums sounded for hours, there were hundreds of floral offerings. 'Mita, Mita,' a woman wailed, 'what is going to happen to us?'

"The spiritual leaders assured everyone that Mita would never leave them. 'The spirit of God never dies. She was the mother every human being wants,' said Mrs. Edith Stiber, a Philadelphia investment broker who joined the sect four years ago.

"A university student commented, 'She studied with my mother in elementary school; oh, it's not possible for her to be a god! People who have no education believe in her.' "

"Her mystery is the mystery of love."

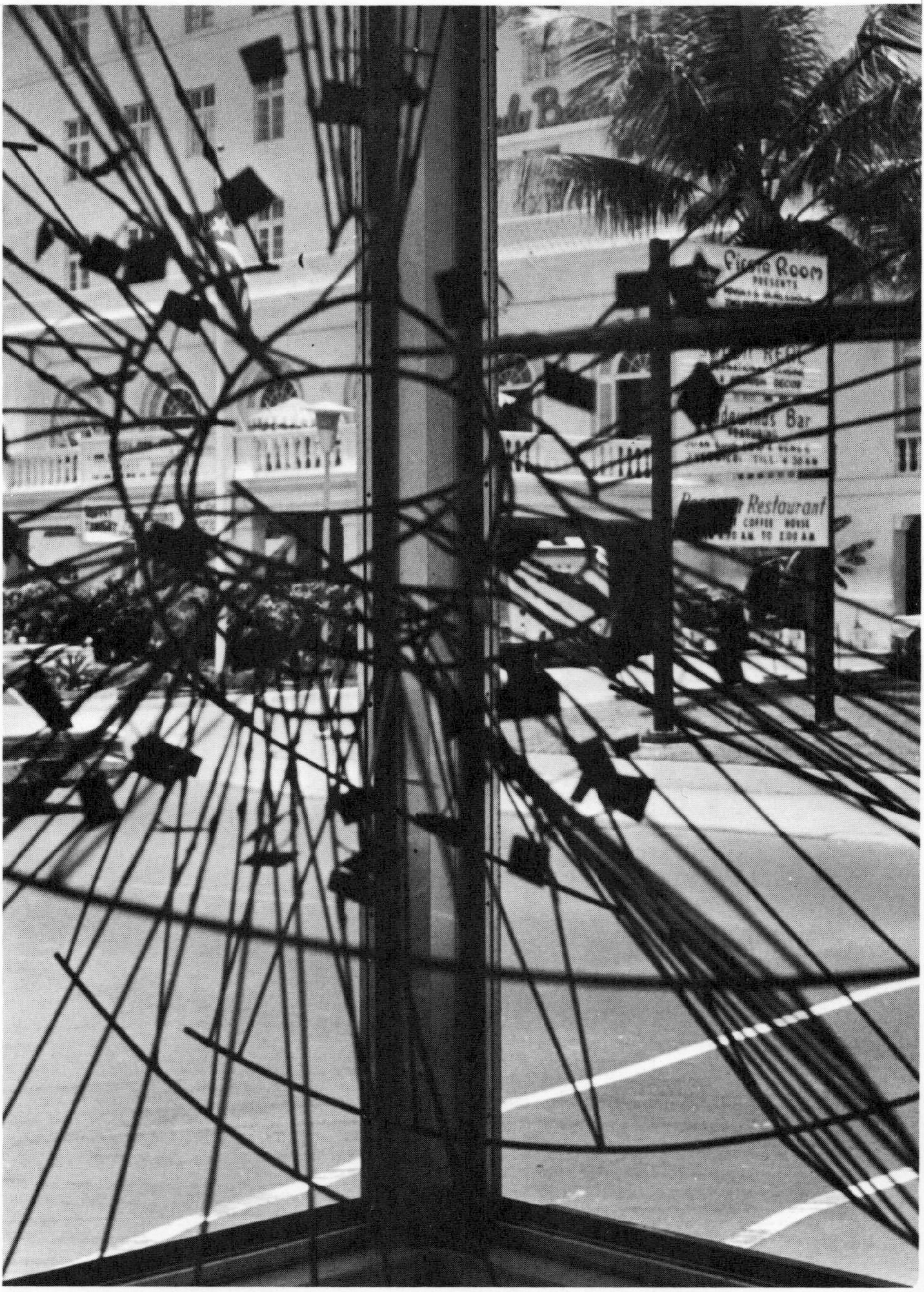

The Condado is a playground for wealthy Americans and Puerto Ricans.

6

San Juan

Modern San Juan is a fast-growing city on the North Shore. Crowded highways lead into the city from all directions. Skyscrapers tower coldly above smaller buildings and dreary stretches of slums. Commercial establishments herald the American presence: Clairol, Sears Roebuck, Grand Union, MacDonald's hamburgers, and Woolworth's.

Modern apartment houses have mushroomed everywhere. Air-conditioned shopping centers entice the shopper to buy American-made items from clothing to comic books. In residential sections of Santurce, Hato Rey, and Río Piedras, stuccoed dwellings house the comfortable middle class.

The Condado, playground for vacationing Americans and their Puerto Rican counterparts, was once an area of coconut groves. Today, the mammoth Miami-style hotels blot out the view of the ocean front reserved for the exclusive use of their clientele. Tourists promenade Ashford Avenue, browsing in elegant shops. In the evening, Latin music is heard in the hotel restaurants and gambling casinos.

The focal point of San Juan is the beautiful fortress city established by Ponce de León in the sixteenth century. There are exquisite plazas, churches, and historic landmarks such as La Fortaleza, the magnificent palace of the governor. Delicate, pastel-colored houses with lovely wrought-iron balconies and gates resemble those of Andalusía, the birthplace of many of the original Spanish settlers.

On the promontory overlooking the Atlantic are the walls of El Morro and San Cristóbal, the sixteenth-century fortresses that for hundreds of years protected the city from English, French, Dutch, and Danish privateers. A bustling Spanish outpost early in the Conquest, San Juan declined during the seventeenth and eighteenth centuries, while the rest of the Island thrived on a brisk and lucrative smuggling trade. When Spain lifted the ban on foreign shipping, in the nineteenth century, San Juan prospered again.

Because of its nostalgic beauty, Old San Juan is the home of artists, poets, and craftsmen, and is a favorite tourist haunt. The finest restaurants, curio shops, boutiques, and night clubs are located here.

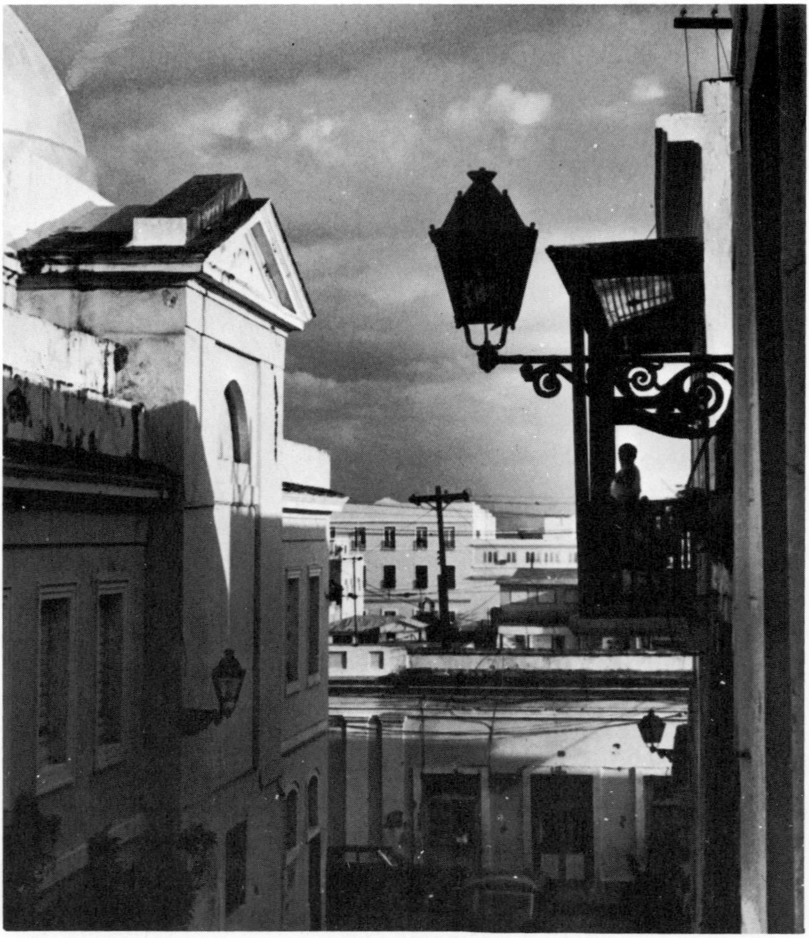

Old San Juan

LA PERLA

La Perla, a barrio of Old San Juan, is a city in miniature. It is a slum, though not the worst—where middle class, poor, and destitute live side by side. Though mulattos and blacks are seen there, La Perla is mainly white. Originally, it was well-to-do, a pearl, as the name suggests; today, only the foundations of good homes and the beautiful cobblestone pavements testify to the affluent past.

In the early 1900's, poor people of Spanish origin left the mountains to settle in La Perla. To be safe from the treacherous tides of the Atlantic, they built their houses close to the wall along the Boulevard, which separates La Perla from adjacent Old San Juan. Their descendants, now middle class, still live there.

Emilio Rodríguez Vásquez, a student at the university who works with the Head-Start program in La Perla, described the barrio: "The more recent arrivals, the very poor, live in filthy houses right on the beach. These were swept away by tidal waves in 1968 and 1970. There is no farm land, because the houses are close together, but the people raise pigs.

"The road entering La Perla leads right from the Boulevard into 'Wipeout,' the worst part of the barrio. This is the place of prostitutes, drug addicts, and drunks. Everybody is in the streets, drinking beer, singing, and dancing. Nobody is rich, but they are not starving either. To smoke marijuana, a 'respectable' man goes surreptitiously to 'Wipeout' or the Boulevard.

"La Perla was long known for its peddlers, who wheeled their carts through the streets while singing the most beautiful songs. Many were blind and sold brooms, whistling to let you know they were coming. There was also a little jewelry shop where you could buy 'hot' watches and jewelry—cheap!

"The poor down at the beach don't pay their rent (the minimum is $10 per month), so they get kicked out. Sometimes they double up with other families for a while and then return. Nobody pays for electricity, except those with meters. Water and electricity are stolen from public pipes.

"Police used to investigate these illegalities but, during the time Felisa Rincón was the mayor of San Juan, she ignored the whole business. There were two thousand votes in that community and she wanted them all! Once in a while, she would send a truck load of food, lollipops for the kids, and shirts for the men. Everyone loved her because she was the only politician who was personally interested in their needs. The new mayor never goes there, and he knows he'll never get La Perla's votes.

"Many families with no father receive welfare assistance. They get powdered eggs and milk, dried meat, butter, huge cans of vegetables, and toilet paper. The butter and milk are very good, but the meat is terrible. They don't need the butter, because they haven't any bread, so they sell it illegally and buy rice and beans.

"The people of La Perla are friendly and help one another out. When a mother deserts her children, someone adopts them. Many women are unmarried and have children with several men. They love animals and have many pets—dogs, cats, and rabbits. They eat chickens, but kids like rabbits, so they don't eat them.

"Even the poor have TV sets. Everybody plays the lottery. Once a fellow won the jackpot and invited hundreds of people to a party. They bought three pigs and roasted them on the beach. Everybody had a great time, but the money was gone when the party was over.

"The priests and nuns in La Perla adapt themselves to the religion of the people, a popular Catholicism. They preach where they like for there are no churches. As elsewhere on the Island, there are many spiritualists."

ANTONIO MARTORELL

Antonio Martorell, now in his thirties, is one of Puerto Rico's respected graphic artists and a leader in social and artistic thought. To conservatives, his long hair and beard mark him as a nonconformist, but he is a charismatic force in the city. Like many other intellectualists, Martorell is an *Independentista,* but he works within the system realistically and constructively. He is director of the Taller Alacrán (Scorpion Workshop) on Cerra Street in Santurce's slum area.

"My grandfather," says Martorell, "came from Majorca, Spain. At the beginning of the century, he started a workshop in Santurce, making beautiful wooden doors and windows. He was a great craftsman, and many people of the barrio learned their trade there. Years later, when I established the Taller, I had his reputation in my favor. He was a great man, a good man, a strong man. At first,

"I don't think we need wonderful artists as much as wonderful people who are artists!"

people questioned my beard, but that was all right because I was the old man's grandson.

"He made a small fortune in the workshop. Of course, my father's generation considered it merely a means of making money. They became part of the upper middle class, and I was to be the culmination of the process. They wanted me to be a doctor; I refused. Then, unsure of myself and trying to please everyone, I went into international relations. They liked that because it was then the dream of Puerto Rico to be a new Greece, a meeting place of Spanish and American culture—all that crap that Governor Muñoz Marín gave us in the 1950's! . . . I soon realized that politics was not for me, and I went into the arts, which had been my first vocation. I studied in Europe, the States, and then in Puerto Rico with Homar, who started me thinking of art as a community project. Lorenzo Homar emigrated to New York as a boy. For a while, he was an acrobat and then served in World War II. Before and after the war, he was trained as a designer in Cartier's [one of New York's leading jewelry stores]. Cartier's had an apprentice system that taught him the entire craft.

"When I met Homar, he was director of the Institute of Culture's graphic workshop. I studied with him there. The Institute already

"Most of the Taller kids . . . have had experience

had workshops in sculpture, graphic arts, and reconstruction of *santos*. We learned while working.

"Later, they set up a school with teachers, classrooms, and grades. The school gives good formal training, and I've no doubt it will produce wonderful artists. It's free and they give scholarships. But —*I don't think we need wonderful artists as much as wonderful people who are artists.* There is a difference. We need people who can work together, who have a duty towards the community, not an academy where individual expression is almighty. That's why I believe workshops are a better way of learning the arts than a school.

"When the Institute refers to popular art and folklore, it means the past. For them, Puerto Rican culture is what the Indians, the Spaniards, and the Africans left us. It's dangerous to talk about what the Americans are leaving us. Besides, most of our elite tend to look at the United States as Coca-Cola culture. They consider themselves spiritually superior to those materialistic Americans, but they only hide their own insufficiencies.

"We are also interested in the past, but we don't put it on a pedestal. The Institute is a showcase for Puerto Rican identity, but everything they do and foster is not wonderful. I'm as Puerto Rican

 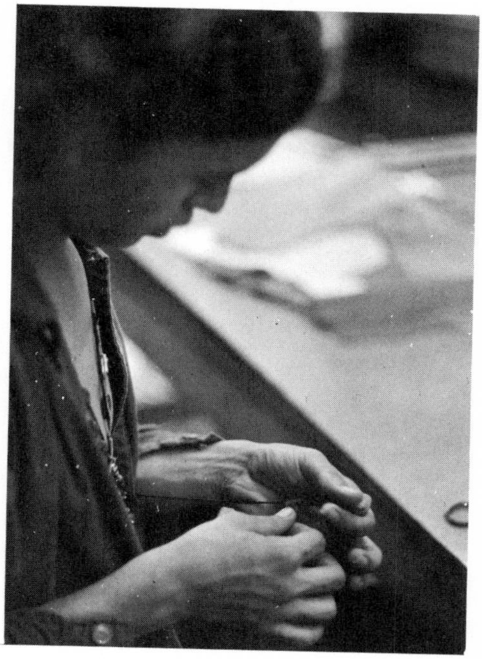

with drugs. But here . . . they say estoy en algo."

as they, but crap is crap, whether it's Puerto Rican or not. Young people reject anything on a pedestal. So do I. We use things from the past in modern ways.

"Right now we're trying to build a Puerto Rican self-image. We must do this because we have always been put down, beginning with the Spaniards, who saw this as a wilderness.

"Most of the kids of the Taller are from the working class. They find strength and self-assurance in doing things together, helping each other. They have no tradition of working alone. When they want to make something on their own, I encourage them. You know what? They'd work alone for an hour or two and then go back to work collectively. The few from the middle class have no problems at all; they just go right back to loneliness and individualism. . . . Recently, when our funds ran out, things got very bad, not because we couldn't pay their food bills but because they couldn't eat together! Ordinarily, fifteen to twenty-five people work and eat together. When that was interrupted—their world collapsed; they didn't know what to do. Working together in the Taller, they had assurance, and an objective. . . . Most of the kids who helped set up the Taller are from nearby or similar neighborhoods. We painted the outside very psychedelic with strong yellow, blue, and orange.

Its looks more like a discotheque than a workshop and got us into trouble with the school principal. The kids were cutting classes to come to the shop! . . . Then we got into trouble because of rumors that the workshop was a center of drug traffic. The principal prohibited the students from coming to us. I was enraged when I heard the news, but luckily, I cooled down and was able to convince her that the Taller wasn't that kind of place. . . . Drugs are dangerous to our very existence. We understand kids looking for escape. We know also that those who work in the Taller don't need drugs. But we can't take addicts. At least 90 per cent of Puerto Rican youth are experimenting with different kinds of drugs. Our experience with heroin addicts and LSD-users has been absolutely heartbreaking for all concerned. . . . Occasionally, we have had trouble from the police. In order to protect ourselves, we formed a Society of Friends of the Scorpion Workshop, to back us with their names and reputations. Some of our people have records of political activism, so the police come snooping around.

"The Taller itself does not go into politics. Sometimes we cold-shower kids when they come in all fiery and rebellious. They resent all authority—family, school, police. As for the church, it is so weak now, they just ignore it. They are Catholics but not practicing Catholics. . . . Once the police picked up Carmelo on the street—said he looked suspicious. They took him to the station and beat him up. I want to the station with a few kids from the Taller and, when I saw his condition, I asked to use the phone. They wouldn't let me, so I started taking down the names of the police. Finally, they threw us all down the stairs. . . . I have good friends in the press and I made a formal complaint to the Civil Service Commission, but the police still try to intimidate us. The poor in our neighborhood are afraid of the police but they understand who we are. They can see for themselves by coming in. There is no mystery about what we are doing. . . . The kids are proud of the Taller and bring their friends. We have never put an ad in the paper. They come on their own. We show them how to make things so that eventually they can earn a living.

"We have difficulty financing ourselves and hope for help from Washington. For a while, we did small jobs, but it didn't even pay our overhead. We can manage only necessities like lodging and clothing but no food, no salaries. I don't get any money, because my wife works. Those who live at home don't get rent money. But orphans and those from out of town get help.

"For decades Puerto Ricans had to get their training in New York, but now we want Puerto Ricans in New York to come *here* for their training and set up workshops in New York. We hope to get scholarships for them. These ideas must come from Puerto Ricans. Just as the black movement in the States emphasizes Africa, we focus on our origins. The hippies here in their communes emphasize Indian communal living and are revitalizing old trades and crafts. We have one thing going for us, however, that black Americans don't have. We have our own piece of land. Despite the American presence, it is still ours. Our people can come back to Puerto Rico from wherever they are, and they do come back.

"The word *maestro* means 'teacher,' but it also means 'master of his craft.' We only have teachers in the latter sense. . . . This is how our education works. We have a guy who, like most of our kids, is a school dropout, a juvenile delinquent, experienced with drugs. He has been in reform school, and his parents have chased him out of the house. He is attracted by the Taller. So he comes, looks around, and we explain what we're doing. We invite him to lunch. By this time he's curious. 'How do I get in?' And they say, 'You just work like the rest of us.' 'I don't know how.' 'Well, you can learn like everybody else. If you need any explanation, just ask, that's what we're here for.' The kid starts learning right away. In two or three days, the Taller is like his home . . . no, not like his home—better than his home! At home he never felt good.

"O.K., let's analyze it. Here, there's no division between student and teacher. Both are involved in work. A lot of my apprentices call me by my first name; they say 'tu' to me. We don't use the 'usted' form. They respect me, but that's the way they express their affection. We have a relationship, without divisions of class, age, attitudes. We have artistic unity, economic unity . . . we share everything.

"Having gone through the regular education system, I am amazed that I managed to learn anything at all. So many teachers don't know as much as they should and are not motivated. Most children go to school because the laws says they have to. Learning is really a miracle when it happens. Here, it is different. People do the things they are interested in."

The Taller Alacrán has received favorable notice in the press. The

"We share everything."

San Juan *Star* calls it "a new concept in learning and neighborhood art" and says, "the streets are never still when Taller Alacrán goes out to practice. People stand and stare as the students sit on the sidewalk and begin to draw."

The Taller makes papier-mâché articles, jewelry, and vases. They have designed wallpaper and printed fabrics—and even playing cards, using caricatures of leading Puerto Rican political figures. It also designs fashions. Martorell often wears a handsome Taller Alacrán suit, a style worn by his grandfather in the Spanish-American War. Many of the Island's best posters are turned out by the Taller. Some of them are destined for New York; one of these was for the Spanish-speaking theatrical troupe Nuevo Teatro Pobre de America, an exciting group of socially conscious actors and playwrights.

Carmelo Martínez, in his late twenties, one of the founders and subdirector of the Taller, and Jorge David Echevarría (called "Rolington" after the Rolling Stones), in his early twenties, talked about themselves and the world they live in. Carmelo was an easel painter before coming to the workshop. A few years ago, he went to Mexico

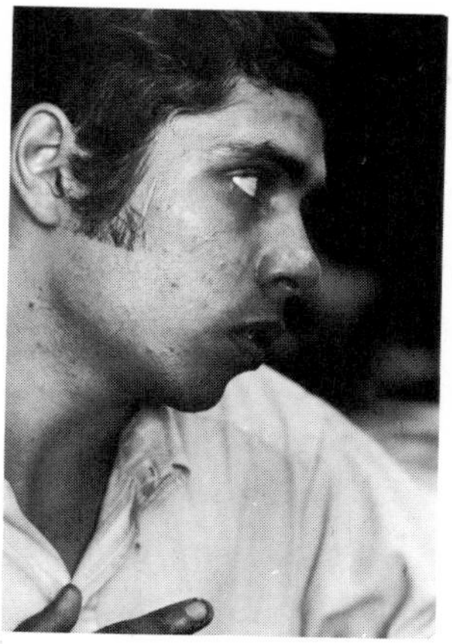

"Everyone wants to belong somewhere."

and was tremendously impressed by the great murals on the walls of public buildings. Back in Puerto Rico, he searched for a meaningful art, one that would have social purpose, and found it in the Taller.

Carmelo: "I was born and raised in Manatí. I came from a very poor class, poor, poor, what they call here *el arrabal* [the slum]. I'm *arrabelero* [colloquial for 'from the slum'], and I have had no artistic traditions in my family. Most of the people in the Taller are very intelligent, with a great deal of potential. They also are very sensitive and easily victimized. They're tired of being rejected in

"A boy dashes out into the street . . . but maybe what he finds is dangerous."

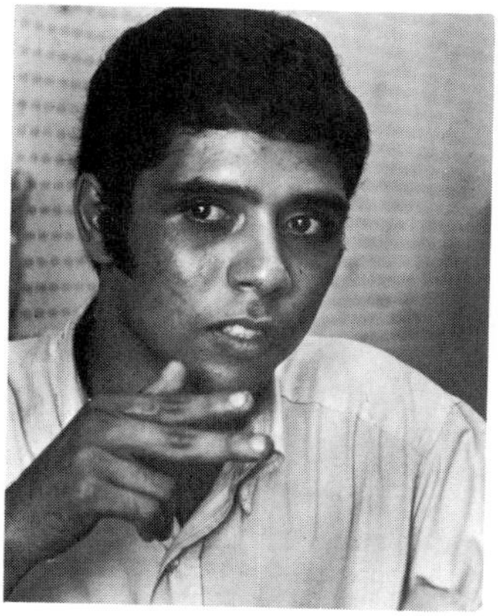

school, so they drop out. It's too much to be told you're dumb and good for nothing if you don't have good grades. Then they tell you that you can't have long hair, because only bandits wear long hair. That's why so many Puerto Rican kids are rebellious."

Rolington: "My family didn't accept my long hair at first, but they didn't say anything, because they know I'm doing something, not just bumming around. In Puerto Rico, hair is for women—they don't accept 'hairy freaks.' My family—I have fifteen brothers—and neighborhood accept me now, but not the school. When I came in with long hair, they told me to cut it. If I didn't, they wouldn't permit me to study. And there I was—out in the street, being clubbed by police!

"I don't go to school now, and I don't believe in the schools we have here. If they taught things that interested me, it would be different. I've always liked literature and reading, but in school they don't encourage you to read. All they give is homework—the useless kind.

"They don't teach us anything about our own country. That we learn by looking around us. They give us propaganda from abroad. They cram it into you but they don't teach. I haven't anything against schools, really, but the ones we have don't teach a thing!

"They tell us about George Washington, Abraham Lincoln, and Armstrong Collins [*sic*], the astronaut. Our book on the history of the United States is huge and well presented. The history book of our own country is a tiny pamphlet and badly written.

"If I had continued school, I'd probably have organized students to revolt against it. If I had to burn the school, I'd burn it! This is the way to study, like we're doing in the Taller."

Carmelo: "Lots of kids leave home because they feel hostile towards their families. In Puerto Rico, church and family are very strong. Subjects like sex are taboo. We don't talk about it. It's simple for a young boy to have sexual hang-ups and explode into homosexuality at the age of sixteen. No wonder they react to sex like animals!

"Most families have terrible problems. Industrialization has affected family life. Parents work and little children are left alone. The father hardly knows his son; the son doesn't know his father. The parents are all involved in their neuroses, and there's no communication. If they speak at all, it's only to fight. The boy dashes out into the street, looking for help. Maybe he finds it, but maybe what he finds is dangerous.

"If a girl leaves home at fifteen, society comes down hard on her. She has the same basic problems as a boy—loneliness and the need for love and sex—but she has to repress her emotions. If she's a rebel, she'll break with that, but everyone will condemn her. Her family will reject her.

"Young people are looking for something, a reaffirmation of life. There are communes for runaway kids. The lawyer looks for his kind; the painter, for his; and so do these forsaken kids. It's human nature. Some become rebels, join youth organizations; some go into politics. But suppose they find vices instead? And what's more available here than drugs? We have a junkie's culture here!

"Everyone wants to belong somewhere, *estar en algo* [to be 'in']. If I smoke 'pot,' then I'm *en algo*. Even though taking drugs is negative, it is a search for something. But that brings many problems. Most of the Taller kids, like most Puerto Ricans, have had experience with drugs. But, here, when they say *estoy en algo*, they mean they have a concrete goal, they are doing something worthwhile. They look at their work and say, 'Goddamn, look what I've done! Wow!' And they're surprised! And they remember how they thought they could invent thirty thousand things with marijuana. Here it takes hard work and discipline to move ahead. But this place is so tiny. If only it could be like this everywhere!

"At least, students can find a sympathetic professor or read Marx and Engels. Not the workers. The bar near our shop is filled every day with workers who can't stand their homes. Immediately after work, they get drunk. When they're drunk, they talk politics. They have no confidence in their government but don't know what to do about it."

Carmelo, like Martorell, has mixed feelings about Americans. "I lived in New York for six months," he said, "then in Denver, San Francisco, and New Mexico. I have many friends in the United States. But New York left a bad impression on me. I had problems getting work, and saw the terrible way my people live there.

"I really love the Mexicans. After my own people, they are closest to my heart; they shared everything with me. But they also live terribly in San Francisco and Denver."

Rolington shares Carmelo's views of Americans but vents his spleen on the military. "I don't like the navy. They're here and so

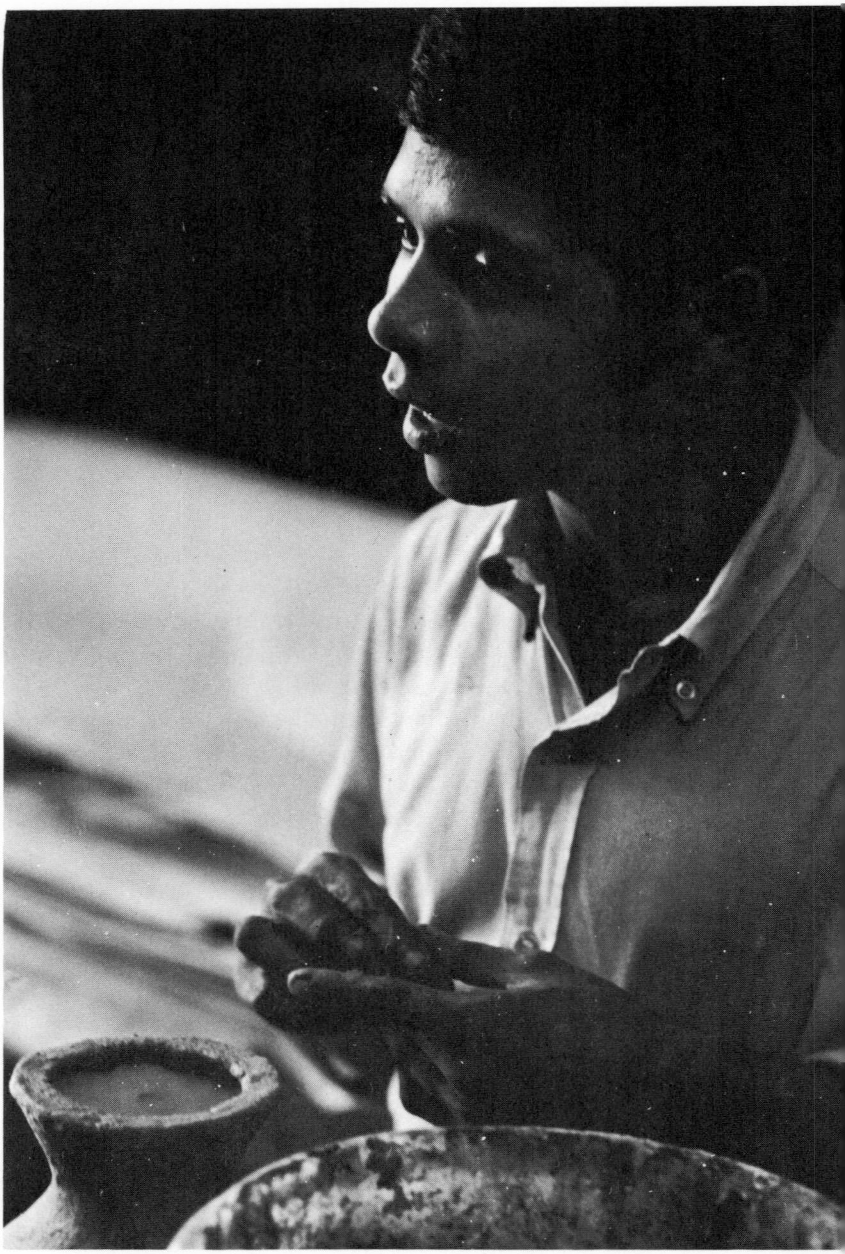

"It's too much to be told you're dumb and good-for-nothing if you don't have good grades."

am I. I would love not to have them here. But what can I do about it? If they call me to the army, I'll see to it that I don't go."

Antonio Martorell talked about Americans and his own people:

"When I was fifteen, I lived in the States with an aunt. I found the loneliness of people in a big city shocking. It is like this all over the world, but in the States it is horrible. I would see people eating alone in restaurants, facing a wall or a mirror. It was so unnatural. . . . not just grabbing a hamburger, but a whole meal, like an animal.

"The second thing that got me was the attitude towards old people. Once I stayed overnight at the YMCA in New York. The next morning, I saw ladies in their seventies, down on their knees scrubbing the floors. I was shocked out of my mind. You don't find that here in Puerto Rico. Never! Old people are taken care of by their sons or grandsons.

"The meaning of death in American culture is different. Death is important to us. That is why spiritualism is popular here. When people go to the spiritualist, they believe they are communicating wth their ancestors. There is continuity. They get messages from them. Death plays a definite role for the living.

"No one here—even in this big city—would dream of taking out burial insurance! When I first heard about it, I said, the U.S. is uncivilized! Here you always have a next of kin, a friend, or a neighbor to bury you, no matter what. Oh, someone in the street might go to a common grave, but it is almost unheard of. *The minute you die, you become sacred!*

"I noticed that Puerto Ricans look different in New York. Our skin is a kind of rich coffee color when we have sun. When we don't, we look like dried nuts, very unpleasant. In the subway I would see my brothers there, without sun, underground, wearing those big overcoats. No matter how well tailored, they looked too big. Our bodies and the way we move in our warm climate are not meant for these clothes. Even if it's a hundred-dollar coat, it always looks *over*coated."

Some Puerto Rican cities and towns are exquisite. Freshly painted houses, well-tended plazas with trees and flower beds give the feeling of well-being and civic pride. Yet Puerto Rican sections of New York, particularly at the end of a sunny weekend, are littered with beer cans and refuse of every description.

Martorell: "Maybe it has to do with the hostility towards the whole place. They just don't care. It's not my house; it's not my society; I don't take pride in this . . . who cares?

"At the bottom of all the different attitudes towards Americans and their government, there is always resentment. You find it even among those who are pro-American, who would love to have been born with blue eyes and blond hair and speak nothing but English.

"In Puerto Rico, we have every shade of opinion on this matter. We have the ultra anti-American who sees nothing good in America, who caricatures America as Coca-Cola culture, goddamn gringos who have come to prostitute us . . . Yankee imperialism unqualified. We have opportunists who would kiss the sidewalk they walk on in order to get something. These people think we should be grateful to be citizens of the United States. You should have seen Ferré when they put the men on the moon! He called the nation to prayer because this *fellow countryman* of ours was on the moon! 'Let us thank the Lord we are part of such a great nation'. . . he was prostrated. But you don't have to sink so low!

"In defending ourselves from Americanization, some people—even revolutionaries—praise their Spanish heritage. They talk about how much better it was in the last century, and the beauties of the language. They even go back to the Indians, back, back, back. Well, *the past is always safe. To go forward is risky.*

"It is very difficult to be objective on this subject. I try to make a difference between the U.S. Government and the American people, and the American people and the American person. I myself have lived in your country, and I have enormous respect for a lot of American ideas, art, painting, and theater. I always have respect for the human being. I am for nationalism, not as an end in itself but as a means to become something."

Martorell feels that it is now time to turn the tables with respect to U.S.–Puerto Rican understanding. "Because you have the money and the power, you can come here and analyze us, subject us to close scrutiny, and then publish your findings. Now I'm working on a project in which our point of view would be emphasized—how Americans look to us, how Puerto Ricans in New York look to us. I'd like to document that in photographs with some text.

"This Island is supposed to be a commonwealth. But we are really a colony. This has been so well disguised that many people resent the word colony. Look around you—we are mostly Puerto Ricans here; there are few Americans. The policeman is Puerto Rican; he has the same color and speaks the same language that we do. The colonial power is *within ourselves.*

"It is really different for the Puerto Rican in New York, just as for the blacks. There you can recognize the enemy . . . there you're pushed against the wall because you are black, because you speak Spanish, because of this or that.

"But things are changing. We feel the pressure, and the suppression is on. Our colonial status is more evident now; *even the press is admitting it.* I think the change in government [Ferré's election] has a lot to do with it."

THE OLDER GENERATION

Americans wonder why some Puerto Ricans seek independence, when the Island receives so many benefits as a commonwealth. In this chapter, respected leaders from many fields offer their views on the subject.

Fred Nasario, Secretary of Labor under former Governor Muñoz Marín, is one of the Island's more astute political observers. Although he is no longer in office, his influence is widespread among intellectuals and people involved in politics.

Question: "Where do the workers of Puerto Rico stand on the issue of Independence or Statehood?"

Nasario: "I would say that less than 1 per cent of the labor force favors Independence. I know every union in Puerto Rico, and not one of them favors it. If they were forced to choose, the majority would certainly take Statehood. But, barring that, most workers would say, 'Let's not force the situation; leave it as it is.' "

Question: "What does Statehood mean to the Puerto Rican laborer?"

Nasario: "Statehood doesn't lure the worker, because he isn't interested in status. He wants a job, better pay, social security, and welfare benefits. He wants to feel free to go to the mainland and work there if he has no work here.

"But if you could prove to him that he would automatically get at least $1.60 an hour or $2.00, like American workers, he'll vote for Statehood.

"The problem is, people don't know what Statehood means. Statehood means that many industries here now would not stay, because the advantages, like low wages and no federal or local tax, would no longer be in effect. [Most United States firms operating abroad have to pay U.S. federal taxes, but not those in Puerto Rico.] Operation Bootstrap [a program of the 1950's, which transformed Puerto Rico's agrarian economy into an industrial one] was successful because Puerto Rico was *not* a state.

"If Puerto Rico becomes a state, we will have to pay federal and local Puerto Rican income tax. In some Southern states, the investor doesn't pay local taxes, only property taxes. In some, he even gets tax exemptions on property as well. In view of this, Puerto Rico would lose its American investors.

"But tax exemptions could be wiped out easily. Our status doesn't have to change. The Internal Revenue Office can knock it off any time they want."

Question: "Could Independence succeed?"

Nasario: "That's completely unknown, but an independent Puerto Rico would need a rearrangement of allies and treaties, of spheres to move into, and a change in industrial growth. We could never keep the present pace going, because it is artificially provoked anyway. The high rate of industrialization has positive aspects but hinders our own initiative.

"In Puerto Rico, we have no civic attitude—of doing something for ourselves. We're completely cynical. I don't blame my people, because in a cynical situation it's the best way to be. What the workers want to know is *what's coming my way?*"

The problem is, people don't know what Statehood means.

Martorell: "But deep inside everyone is the question of status. There are moments in everyone's life—even Statehood and pro-government people—when it burns you that you are not your own man, that this is not your own country or your own destiny. And the more drinks, the more you'll hear, 'I am an *Independentista* at heart, you know.' At four o'clock in the morning in Puerto Rico, Independence would win by a landslide."

Nasario: "The success of an independent Puerto Rico depends on the United States. Right now, our surplus population is absorbed through migration to the mainland. But, if, with Independence, that flow should stop, then Puerto Rico would be like Jamaica and Trinidad—with about 25 per cent unemployment.

"Now, if the U.S. said, 'All right, you can come freely to the States for fifty years until you adjust yourselves,' well, that might be different. We cannot absorb the surplus into our economy now. Puerto Rico is the most heavily populated area for its size in the whole U.S.A.

"Some old-timers say we are Spanish, totally Spanish, here, but we are completely dependent on the United States. Everything has come from the United States—progress, money, education, well-being."

Milton Pabón, head of the Department of Political Science at the University of Puerto Rico, like many of his colleagues, is an *Independentista.* A handsome, quiet man in his forties, he was educated in the States, and speaks fluent English.

Señor Pabón observes, "Puerto Rico is a commonwealth; however, the literal translation in Spanish is *estado libre asociado* (free associated state). But it is not a state, not free, and not associated. The commonwealth status granted us in 1952 by the United States Congress was a way of making our colonial regime more palatable. It allows us to enact our own constitution with the following guidelines: We must keep a republican type of government; we cannot regulate federal policy on military service, our own status, immigration, commerce, or communications. The only improvement since 1900 was a Congressional act in 1947, allowing us to elect our own governor, who appoints his own cabinet. Previously, the President of the United States appointed the governor. . . . You can point to economic growth in Puerto Rico but not to political growth. We are in a colonial situation. We are given the impression that we have our own constitution, our own autonomy and democratic regime. But it is not so."

Said a student, "A colony is a place where the real power is outside the limits of the territory. In the case of Puerto Rico, the real power is not our Senate but the Congress of the United States!"

Like many Puerto Ricans, Señor Pabón sees Statehood as the end of his country as a separate entity: "It means death—and why should the United States give us Statehood when they are getting what they want right now without us interfering in *their* affairs.

"What do they want? They want military bases; they want to send Puerto Ricans to Vietnam; and they want us as a market. They also want to use Puerto Rico to justify their own foreign policy. And Puerto Ricans, especially politicians, play the game and sell themselves cheaply."

Señor Pabón commented on the relation between political status and education: "Our Department of Education does not have national goals. All over the world, children are educated to be citizens of their country: in the United States, to be Americans; in France, to be French; in Germany, to be German. Perhaps that's not the ideal thing but, until we live in a world not divided into nations, human beings must be educated to be something, to belong somewhere, to have a certain security. That security we do not have in Puerto Rico.

"Eleven or twelve different school systems have been tried since 1898 to make Puerto Ricans bilingual. They thought it would be easy, but it isn't. English is important, but we are a Spanish-speaking nation. We have common traditions, as well as a common tongue, which we share with more than twenty Latin American countries. We are more like Venezuelans, Colombians, Argentinians, and Cubans than Americans. The United States tries to isolate us from that heritage and impose an alien culture. But nobody wants to be educated to be what one is not.

"Did you know that a law was passed in 1945 allowing us to teach in Spanish? How tragic that a country has to make laws to teach its own language in its own country! The terrible part is that it won in the district courts but lost in the Supreme Court by a technicality. How did we impose Spanish? Administratively!"

"Here's an example of the Americanization process: About a year ago, Walgreen's drugstores were remodeled, and all their signs were changed into English. *Jabón* became soap, *algodón* became cotton,

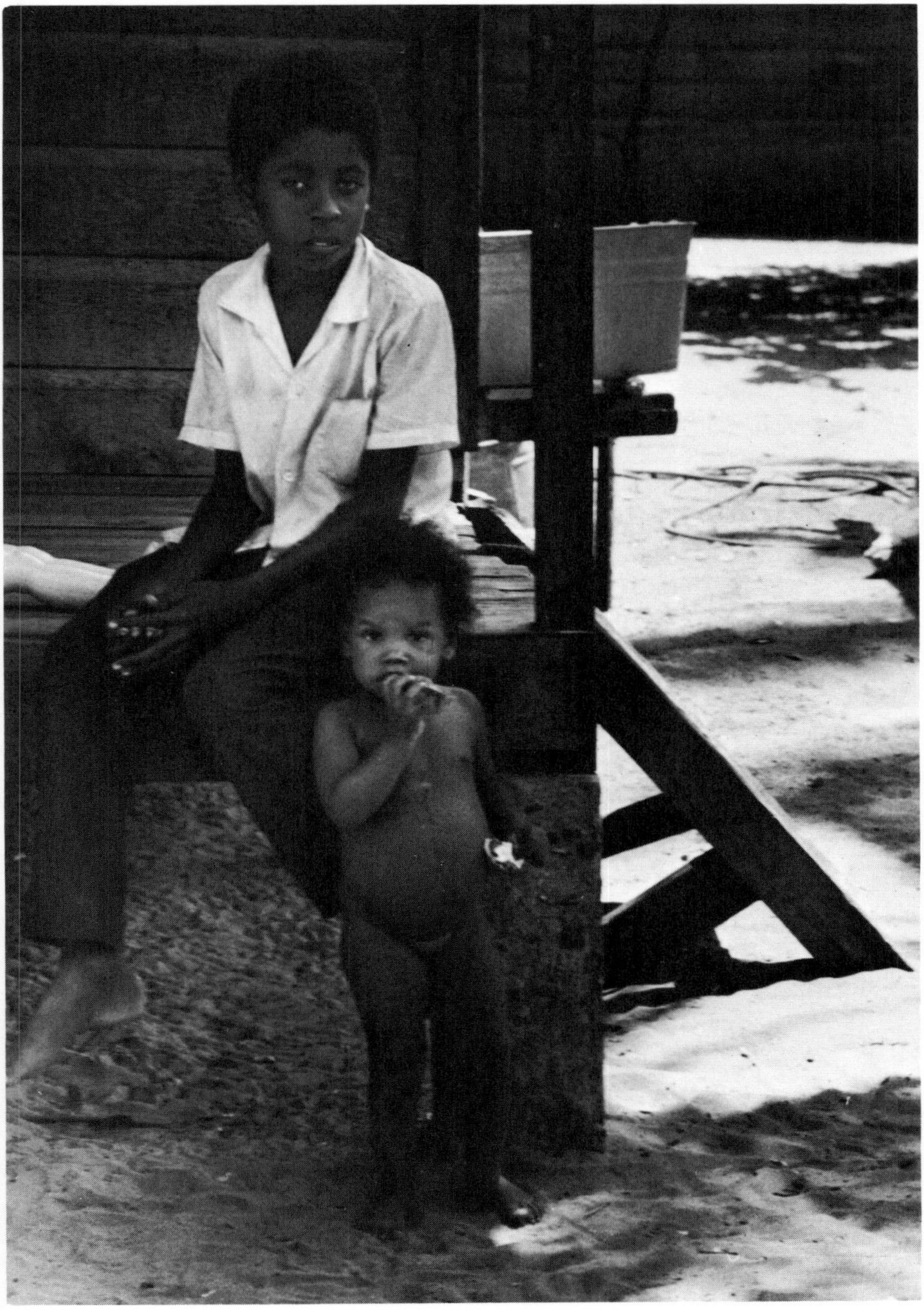

Human beings must be educated to be something, to belong somewhere.

and so on. I bet that if you asked the people going in and out what was new there, most of them wouldn't know!

"This is how far we have gone without Statehood. Imagine what it would be like with Statehood. We'd probably have to become Americanized by a certain date!

"The worst aspect of colonialism is our cultural isolation. True, this is changing, but not fast enough. For example, we are one hour from Caracas by plane, and we don't even know Caracas. We are not only ignorant of Latin America; we are completely prejudiced. We have absolutely no connection with the rest of Latin America. This is colonial-style education. First isolate the people and educate them to be colonized. Then you can dominate them."

There are efforts to remedy this situation. A few artists have been to Mexico, and Ivan Illich's school in Cuernavaca (a famous resort town south of Mexico City) has attracted many students. Some go to Cuba. These are the radical youth for whom Che Guevara and Fidel Castro are the heroes of this age.

Pabón: "The constant coming and going between Puerto Rico and New York also facilitates the Americanization process. Bayamón and Santa Juanita, near San Juan, are purely extensions of the Bronx. Everywhere, you see signs in a mixture of Spanish and English, like Santa Juanita Laundry, or *Come y Vete,* a restaurant sign that might mean 'Come and Go' or 'Eat and Go.' [The word *come* in Spanish means 'eat.']

"Puerto Ricans go to the United States, and Cubans, Americans, Virgin Islanders, Colombians, and Dominicans come here. The Dominicans, poorest of all, work as gasoline attendants and domestics. Both they and the Virgin Islanders come as migrant workers to cut cane and work on coffee and pineapple plantations. Most of them return home after their contracts are concluded. Puerto Rico claims to be overpopulated; yet it imports agricultural workers. The reason? Puerto Ricans prefer industrial and construction work. City life and higher pay are more attractive than long hours on the farm!

"The majority of immigrants to the Island are middle-class and professional people from Cuba and the States. According to some figures, there are thirty to forty thousand Cuban exiles here. Many of our own professionals are threatened by the competition. These Cubans are active in business, construction, land speculation, in mass media and advertising.

"The Cubans in Puerto Rico are very conservative, very pro-

American. They supported Ferré economically—and now are trying to make Communism an issue here, which it is not. If they had the opportunity, I think they would push us Puerto Ricans out. They are arrogant because they know the American Government protects them.

"We have a large American community too, about one hundred thousand. The Cubans and Americans quickly become voters. United and conservative, very anti-anything-which-sounds-liberal, this combination is a strategic and active group whose voting strength is decisive in elections."

A ride through Puerto Rico's Levittown, built by the American real estate developer, reminds one sharply of similar sights in the United States—treeless streets, neat rows of houses in dull, Ameri-man-industrial architectural style. Many Puerto Ricans returning from the States settle in such projects.

Señor Pabón described the pervasive American influence: "Puerto Rican life is U.S.-oriented. The mass media, TV, magazines, leading newspapers (San Juan *Star, El Mundo, El Imparcial*), the products in supermarkets, drugstores, department stores, and shopping centers provide no alternative to the American way of life. The buyer would probably be antagonized if you tried to give him anything else. It has become his way of living too!

"People believe that everything American is superior. In a way, they are saying that they themselves are no good. This is the worst aspect of colonialism. I can only compare it with, for example, the Negro situation in the United States. I always remember Malcolm X's description of a painful experience getting his hair straightened to make him appear less Negro."

Question: "Is there racism in Puerto Rico?"

Ellen Hawes [an American living in Puerto Rico]: "Puerto Ricans say there is color prejudice here, but it is totally different from the States. A black man is served at any hotel or restaurant. Some say, 'You can bring them home to dinner, but I won't let my daughter marry one of them. . . . I won't take them to my club, but I'll vote for them for senator.' "

Nasario: "Oh, yes. It really depends on class. Among workers and even the lower middle class, there is intermarriage between dark and light people. The higher you move, the more prejudice."

Peter Hawes: "The working class jokes about these things, but prejudice is there nevertheless. It's much easier for a successful

Negro to marry a poor white than vice versa. But time will take care of that problem. Because of so much intermarriage, the Negro population is disappearing. There are only pockets of blacks to be found."

Martorell: "We're always comparing our color problem to the States. There it's brutal and bestial, but it doesn't mean we don't have one. Prejudice is very strong and I have felt it in my own family, among my neighbors and friends, in my school, everywhere!"

Fred Nasario discussed the feelings towards Puerto Ricans in New York. "We feel they are different. Some people here don't regard second generation 'Ne-Yoricans' as Puerto Ricans at all, although some of them are beginning to look to their Puerto Rican heritage.

"The most successful Puerto Ricans in the States don't want to be called Puerto Ricans. They call themselves Spanish and move to the suburbs. They could help their own people, but they go away. Those who remain in the cities are the poor, the darker Puerto Ricans.

"Every Puerto Rican knows he is looked down upon, but the more educated deny they are discriminated against. They say, 'I go to college, I work, and I am accepted just like other Americans!' To be 'like all other Americans' is probably what is at the bottom of the sentiment for Statehood in Puerto Rico. Upper- and middle-class Puerto Ricans think their feeling of inferiority can be overcome if they have equal political status—be a State in the Union.

"But workers are discriminated against because of color. Our labor force is dark-skinned. All the federal figures on wages, education, and housing show that as a group the Puerto Rican is on the lowest rung of the economic ladder, even below the blacks. Unfortunately, there is a total absence of pride in our Negro past: Whiteness is the ideal in Puerto Rico.

"Many Puerto Ricans feel vulnerable to attacks and slander on their national character."

Nasario recalled his automatic response to John F. Kennedy's assassination: "I hoped it was not a Puerto Rican. Later, I was in New York when the news of Bobby Kennedy's shooting came. Immediately, I called the governor's office in Puerto Rico, and we checked through the FBI to find out who the man was. An earlier report in New York had insinuated that the killer was a Puerto

Eleven or twelve different school systems have tried to make Puerto Ricans bilingual. But theirs is a Spanish-speaking nation.

Rican. Within twenty minutes, we heard, 'No, it's not a Puerto Rican.' If it had been, we would immediately have gone on the air to quiet the thing down."

Nilita Vientos Gastón, a brilliant literary critic, is an ardent *Independentista.* Tiny, magnetic, eccentric in appearance, bold in public actions and speech, she is a tower of strength. The door of her beautiful book-filled home is always open to those who need her. She has strong opinions on current affairs:

"The Puerto Rican is an American citizen, but *what kind* of citizen? A citizen who doesn't enjoy all the rights or privileges. Why were we given that citizenship? Only to take us to their wars, nothing else! Your government says to us, 'you are a tiny country; you are poor—and this is war.' But why the hell should a country that has never fought for itself fight other people's wars? And what kind of a war is this? A shameful war! The same country that has put men on the moon—such a marvelous thing—is murdering people in Vietnam. Incredible!

"Many draft cases have been brought to court. You need courage to fight the system here. But almost all those who have protested the war have been *Independentistas*. They don't want to fight the war for the Americans."

About the importance of women, she is very definite: "Women do just about everything in Puerto Rico. They are much more important in literature and politics than in the United States. We almost have a matriarchy. For example, for fifteen years, I was director of the Ateneo de Cultura Puertorriqueña, (Atheneaum of Puerto Rican Culture) our oldest cultural institution. I was the first woman to hold the post. I directed the most important literary review. I was also the Attorney General for some years.

"There are women in every position, the Secretary of Labor now is a woman; there are women mayors, women legislators, women doctors, women dentists. Some of the most respected persons in the university are women. In the last few generations, this development has been extraordinary.

"Attitudes on sex and morals change more slowly. Now a father accepts the fact that his daughter is a lawyer or a doctor, but that

Women do just about everything in Puerto Rico.

she makes love to a man she's not married to—that's terrible. There are lots of unmarried couples, but people make believe they're not there. The very rich and the very poor have always done whatever they wanted. It's the middle class that's all mixed up. A poor woman may have five sons with different men, and nobody cares, but no middle-class woman could get away with that without being severely criticized by the community."

Concerning America's cultural impact on Puerto Ricans, she observes, "A powerful country exerts an extraordinary influence on other cultures. Spain had her time. When France was powerful, all cultivated people learned French as their second language. Today it is English because the United States plays such an important political role. From the economic point of view, it is the biggest and most powerful nation in recorded history.

"The Americans feel free *in their country;* we do not feel free *in ours.* That's the mentality of those who have been dominated by others! The Puerto Rican Constitution had to be approved by the United States Congress. What kind of a constitution is it that has to be approved by another country? So, we have two anthems, two flags, two constitutions, two languages, two legal systems (the Spanish Civil Code based on codified law and the Anglo-Saxon based on jurisprudence). We are, as one of our poets said, '*Puerto Rico: Burundanga* [a mixture of everything].' "

A professor of literature at the University of Puerto Rico, Nilita Vientos is a knowledgeable critic of the system of higher education. Her criticism is directed at fundamentals. "Our university is not a Puerto Rican university for Puerto Ricans but a *North American university* for our youth. It has all the defects of the American institutions plus our own. Students here, because of our colonial status, are much more conservative, less revolutionary than students in the United States.

"Our university is a political instrument, a political playground, dominated by the governor with the consent of Congress. That's why we are constantly fighting. For a while, Ferré's son was the president of the Council. Criticism was so overwhelming, he had to resign. Then they assigned another pro-Statehood man! So the fight is over who has the power—the assimilationists or the Puerto Ricans.

"The university needs a transformation. It has been dominated by an outmoded theory of the university as a house of studies. Jaime

Benítez, the rector, who postulated the idea after a student strike in 1948, advocates that college students must live in an ivory tower, removed from the outside world. A stupid thing because our graduates are the directors of our society! They are judges, attorney generals, government officials, and leading businessmen. The self-made man is the exception today.

"We have always had the student demonstrations, but they are few. Right now, they're still discussing in the Council of Higher Education whether to permit picketing on university grounds. Most parents want their children to go to school, get a diploma, and not be involved in anything!

"If I had a son in college and he wasn't involved, I'd get him out of there! I believe a person receiving a college education has the moral responsibility to protest when he sees things are wrong. Otherwise, what good is it to him!"

FATHER FREIXEDO

Some of the most vocal advocates of social and political change in Puerto Rico have come from the Catholic clergy. The publication of *Mi Iglesia Duerme* (*My Church Sleeps*) by a dissident Jesuit priest, the Reverend Salvador Freixedo, raised a storm in the summer of 1969. Father Freixedo took a radical position on many of the controversial issues that have been rocking the Catholic world.

Angered by his insubordination, the Archbishop of San Juan, Luis Aponte Martínez, summarily dismissed Father Freixedo. When this autocratic action drew protest, the church granted Freixedo an opportunity to recant but not to defend himself. Some hierarchy and laity publicly denounced him, but Freixedo received strong support from professionals, university students and faculty, priests, and nuns. He addressed many cheering, standing-room-only audiences. Freixedo's words were not new or startling. Similar criticism had often been leveled at the church, but his had come at the right time. "Greater than the tread of mighty armies," said Victor Hugo, "is an idea whose time has come."

Salvador Freixedo was a tall, handsome man of thirty-seven. His pale, sensitive face and gentle pensive manner suggested a man of thought rather than a man of action. Yet he was both. For more than a decade, he had served with distinction as founder and counselor of the Young Christian Workers, a labor-oriented Catholic action group in Puerto Rico.

In a newspaper interview shortly after publication of *Mi Iglesia Duerme,* he said the following:

"After a great struggle within myself I decided to say exactly what I think should be said. If Jesus Christ came down to earth right now, he couldn't be a Christian. He would not be able to find . . . brotherly love—which would imply that the Church, whose mission it is to spread that message, has failed miserably. . . . Two thousand years make you very wise, but also quite sclerotic. During that time, the Church has built an empire but has forgotten the spirit.

"We take care of those who come to church—mostly well-to-do and middle class and the very few heroic poor who come to Mass. But the very poor are too busy trying to find their next meal to go to church. But yes, we remind them that they must attend Mass every Sunday under pain of mortal sin that sends them to hell! How the blazes are we going to threaten with a hell in the hereafter those who are already living it here right now!"

Commenting on the ban against birth-control, Freixedo wryly said, "It is completely clear that papal encyclicals are not infallible . . . and in the past popes took stands that are today plainly inadmissible." He is confident the church will eventually alter its position on this issue.

Freixedo advocates that marriages be terminated when two people "turn their home into a hell and deform the minds of their children."

On the subject of marriage for priests, he said, "That is not fundamental. The real question is not [so much] whether priests should be allowed to marry as when married men . . . will be ordained as priests."

Freixedo stated that the church, overly preoccupied with sex, makes it the central consideration of many of its positions.

"If we read the Gospel, we find that Christ sees more danger in money than in sex. His admonitions about money are more severe than those about sex. After all, sex isolated is a deformity of love. But money hardens our hearts, makes us selfish—and selfishness is anti-love, and, therefore, the real sin."

Father Freixedo was not sure if the church would prevent him from working within the fold. "If I don't do these things, someone else will. And they cannot silence the entire world."

When asked how he lost his fear, he replied, "By getting to know the poor up close."

STUDENTS

Enclosed by high iron fences, the University of Puerto Rico campus in Río Piedras is a green oasis bordered by busy avenues and slum and middle-class residential areas. Within the campus are well-tended lawns, flowering shrubs, and huge trees heavy with foliage. At night, the song of the *coquí* [tiny frog] is heard.

Inside the Student Center, fraternities and sororities recruit members. Posters announce dances, club meetings, films, and chess tournaments. Students line up at long rows of telephones, most of which operate fitfully, if at all.

Downstairs in the vast cafeteria, students, trays in hand, elbow their way through the crush to crowded tables. Bearded students are in the minority. Everyone is well dressed and groomed. The girls wear fashionable dresses and elegant Spanish shoes. Despite the heat, many wear stockings.

In this prosaic atmosphere, a ferment has been seething. The 1969–70 school year opened with a strike against an insignificant rise in cafeteria prices. The issue, unimportant in itself, revealed the student mood. The day Father Freixedo lectured on campus, the student-center hall was filled beyond capacity long before the appointed hour, and the lecture had to be relocated. The hall emptied in a few minutes, and thousands of students rushed to the huge amphitheater, filling that so there was standing room only.

On the information desk at the student center were strike directives, calls for demonstrations against the Vietnam war and for abolition of the ROTC, and announcements of organization meetings. Pro-Independence publications such as *Guasábara* and *Claridad* suddenly became openly available.

Although not legally recognized by the administration, a number of political organizations function on campus: the most active, FUPI (pro-Independence), AUPE (pro-Statehood), and *Rescate* ("Redemption"—Socialist-Christian).

There are many different groups in the Independence movement. PIP (Partido Independencia Puerto Rico) is a middle-class group favoring voting to achieve Independence. MPI (Movimiento Pro-Independencia) is the most radical group. In addition, there are

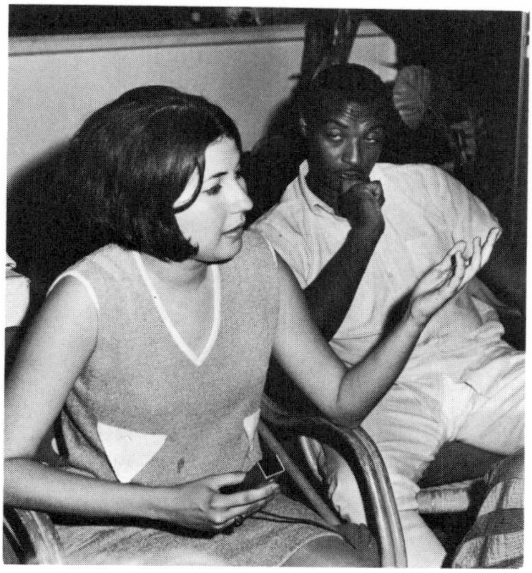

Puerto Ricans say their country has color prejudice, but it is totally different from in the States.

PUP (a splinter group of the PIP), FEPI (high school students for Independence), and CAL (Comandos Armados de Liberación—a small, armed sabotage group).

In the fall of 1969, violence erupted on campus. The small ROTC building was partially destroyed by students. The following March, the main ROTC building was badly burned. Riot police were called in by the university president, Jaime Benítez. Then came a long series of incidents: demonstrations, hunger strikes, fires, bombings, battles with the police—and death.

On November 7, 1969, right-wing students, parents, and anti-Castro Cubans attacked the national headquarters of the MPI after

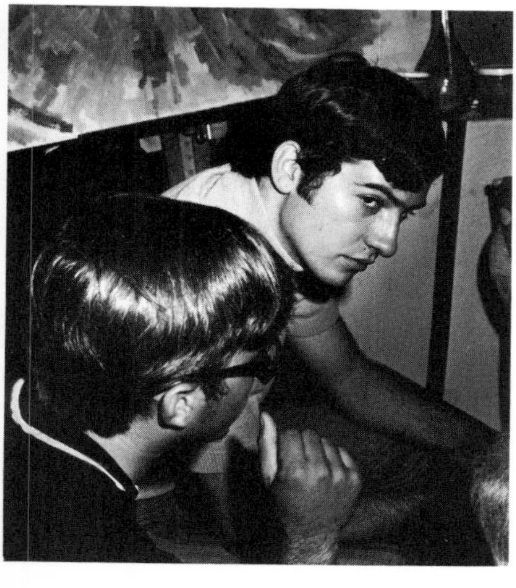

The Puerto Rican is an American citizen, but what kind of citizen?

a demonstration in support of the ROTC. Three people were wounded in the fight. The MPI leaders claimed that the police not only did not help them but actually organized and directed the hostile activities and destroyed paintings, furniture, and other MPI property.

Several weeks later, a huge demonstration was held against compulsory military service. In February, 1970, the offices of *Claridad*, a pro-Independence newspaper, were destroyed by fire.

The most serious incident occurred during an antiwar demonstration on campus in March, 1970, when a young student, Antonia Martínez, was shot to death by the police. According to a Vietnam veteran who was standing at her side, a number of students were on the balcony of a student residence when students pursued by the police came running to them for help. All but one escaped. The police pounced on him and beat him. This brought an angry exchange of words with the police, who, apparently without warning, fired into the balcony, killing young Antonia, grazing the neck of the veteran with the same bullet.

A storm of protest swept the university. The students declared a strike, and demands for Benítez's resignation were heard from radical students and faculty. The police claimed they had no guns, despite photographic evidence to the contrary. This incident served to widen the breach between the government and students.

Many students are very much concerned with the issue of political status. "Why are so many people satisfied with things as they are?" asked one student. Several of his fellows answered his question:

Student A: "The idea of Independence is strong among our people, but they have been asleep and are just now awakening from a lethargic dream."

Student B: "I blame Muñoz Marín for many things. He betrayed us. He told us Puerto Rico was going to be the link between two civilizations, Spain and the U.S. What bull! He used the Independence votes to rise to power. When he got to the top, he changed his mind and said, 'First we must be autonomous. Later on we will have Independence.' Well, we are still waiting!

"When we were a Spanish colony, we fought for autonomy and finally won it. For five months we were autonomous. Then came the Spanish-American War, and the Americans 'liberated' us. But, you know, we were more independent with our autonomy than we are now!"

Student C: "In my opinion, Puerto Ricans are afraid of the consequences of Independence. Most commonwealth-supporters are fundamentally *Independentistas.* When the moment arrives, the people of Puerto Rico will lose that fear and act for their own benefit.

"But people are not ready for that decision. There are too many taboos, like Communism. People are always comparing Cuba to Puerto Rico. Statehood people say, 'If Independence comes, there'll be Communism,' and they say it as if it's an undeniable fact.

"But they have no reason to be afraid. We've never had a war here. It's a phony issue. We talk of war, but we do nothing; besides, they'd eat us alive. You know what we are? A people with an inferiority complex."

Student D: "I tell you there is repression here. I know it because I see it. My father is an *Independentista,* my mother is an *Independentista,* and so am I. Try to get a job with the government; they find out who you are and put you on the black list. Or they accuse you of being Communist or a this or a that."

ROTC student: "I used to belong to a pro-Statehood group at the university, but I left because I didn't think the military had any business in politics. I approve of the war because Communist China is going to take over the world if we don't defend it in Vietnam. Lots of students disagree with me, but I say the United States *is* fighting to preserve democracy. I would like to see a united North and South America run by a strong government but not by the military, because they make machines out of men.

"During my basic training in Southern army camps, I had lots of experiences with white cadets. It was rough in the beginning because nobody would help me. Little by little, I made friends, mostly with blacks. I noticed the white cadets didn't like that.

"One day, I was walking with a few friends when a white cadet threw a pail of dirty dishwater on us. I finally figured it was a guy from Alabama. One night after a platoon party, I saved a little beer in a trash can and waited for him at his bunk. As soon as he came in, I threw it at him and not only wet him but his bunk and his luggage as well. I ran back to my bunk, and pretty soon he came.

" 'Aha!' he said, 'it was you!'

" 'Yes,' I said, 'an eye for an eye and a bath for a bath!'

Students in Puerto Rico are much more conservative than students in the United States.

"I wasn't scared even though he was tougher and bigger, and I was sure I'd beat him in a fight. But he changed and we became friends. Before he left the camp, we had a beer together, and I told him what I thought about people who didn't like blacks. He was embarrassed. At the beginning of camp, he didn't like Puerto Ricans either. I hope he has a different view now.

"There were other things, too, like the time I was in North Carolina with some white cadets. A few black girls passed by, and I complimented them. The cadets gave me a funny look, as if I had spoken to a dog or something. It really bothered me.

"When camp ratings were passed out, the black guys and myself got the lowest points. Maybe it's because I was friends with them. The ratings were based on personal reasons, because those blacks were pretty good cadets!

"We have feelings here, not only the Puerto Ricans but the Dominicans, too. They really hate Americans, and you can't blame them for having a revolution. We feel the Americans are two-faced hypocrites. They put on a good face if they can get something out of you but, when you turn your back, they put on a different face, mostly against you. I think it's mostly business. Lots of Americans come here to take advantage of us. They pay the lowest salaries they possibly can. They don't have a conscience about Puerto Ricans; they only have a conscience for their pockets."

Student A: "The question isn't are we for or against the United States. *The question is: Who am I?* I don't feel American. I am a Puerto Rican completely. But we live under U.S. laws, and I don't feel any obligation to serve that country and army. And in a war like this . . . !"

Another student said, "Independence will not be ushered in by any one political party but by all the people of Puerto Rico."

Like their counterparts in the United States, Puerto Rican students want their university to be responsive to the temper of our times and desire a greater role in policy-making decisions. Here are typical comments:

Student F: "For the first time there is dialogue among students, faculty, and the dean. Perhaps it is only to keep the students quiet, but we are making recommendations, and we hope something will be done."

Student B (natural sciences): "This department is the most politically apathetic in the university. It is in terrible condition. You should see our laboratories; they go back to the fifteenth century! We have good scientific minds, people genuinely interested, but they are being badly prepared by the university for work in Puerto Rican industry. Then foreign experts are hired to fill jobs that Puerto Ricans could do!"

Student A (languages): "Our first readers are English books, like *This Is My Country.* And what do you see? Mountains in Michigan or some other place in the States! The little Puerto Rican boy who reads that kind of book thinks he's in the United States!

"Until 1940, all education was in English. My father told me that, every morning, school kids had to salute the American flag and pledge allegiance to the United States.

"Today, English is a secondary language in all public schools, as it should be. People think we are against English, but we're not. We want good methods and teachers. The poor student in public school learns miserable English; those in private schools do better. In the university, everyone must read and listen to lectures in English, so those who can't have a terrible time. Unfortunately, our own language is degenerating. We mix English and Spanish and don't speak good Spanish *or* English.

"We want to know other languages. We have professors here from all over the world, but they all lecture in English because they don't know Spanish. And what good is that if so many can't get along in English!"

Student B (humanities): "Puerto Rican history is taught in this department. Most professors stop at the twentieth century. We had a strike, and now we have been promised a complete history, including a special contemporary course. We also want courses in psychology and sociology with Puerto Rican rather than American orientation. The same thing goes for cultural studies. One of our classes, Society and Culture in Puerto Rico, is given by an American, and what he talks about *least* is Puerto Rico!"

One of the goals of radical student youth is to effect social change by working with the poor. In the past few years, student communes have been set up in slum areas of San Juan to educate the people to help themselves because "the government will in the end betray you, especially this government." Mostly from the middle class, the students involved have been working on problems of drugs, housing, and justice in the courts.

Among the founders of activity in the slums were students and members of Cine-Pueblo [People's Films], a group making social documentary films. Some work has been done in El Caño de Martín Peña (The Channel of Martín Peña), a San Juan slum, Cataño and Fajardo. One of the first groups to initiate work in the slums was VESPRA (Volunteers in Service to Puerto Rico), part of a government program to aid the disadvantaged, the equivalent of VISTA in the States. Like Legal Services, Inc., it has probably gone beyond the original program, and its members also have been called "Communists" and "dumb dupes."

Student E (slum worker): "Help for slum projects also comes from private sources and from *Independentistas*. We know a prominent lawyer who gives most of his earnings to work in Vietnam, a barrio of Cataño. He also contributes money to a small mimeographed newspaper, *El Cañonazo* [The Sound of a Cannon], published by workers in El Caño de Martín Peña.

"When there is no money, some of us steal, but we consider it a political act. We 'acquire,' you might say, not 'steal.' We take food and clothes from the big shopping areas and American-owned supermarkets. We keep just enough for ourselves and give the rest to the people. But we are against begging and try to convince the people not to do degrading things like that. We organize our activi-

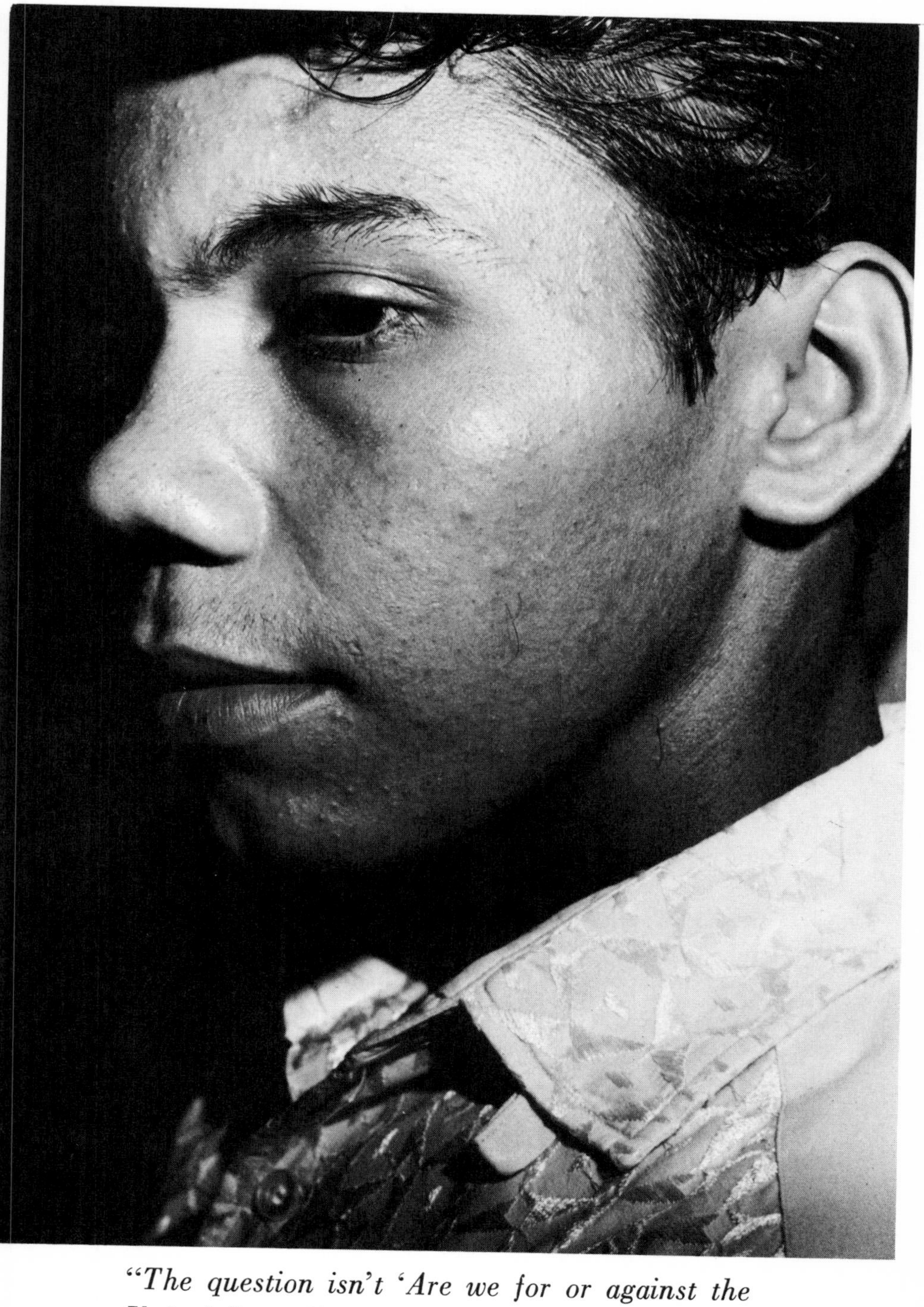

"The question isn't 'Are we for or against the United States?' The question is 'Who am I?' "

ties well but try to keep the names of the students secret. There are always police snooping, but the people defend us and warn us when they are around. We have found many intelligent people in the slum areas. They may be ignorant—uneducated—but they are very bright and willing to cooperate."

Student F: "In the slums, we go alone or in pairs. We say to the people, 'Look, we want to help you. Can we stay the night here?' And the people say, 'Sure.' It's incredible the way we are accepted, because generally people are distrustful of strangers, especially those with good clothes and money in their pockets. We eat with the families, we bring a little something, but we try to make the people understand they are not buying our services. This approach has been so successful that in a few days we have started a community action. It's easy to unite them when everything is against them and everyone is in the same boat."

Student G: "There are other communes in Puerto Rico, but they're like the ones in the States. This is where American and Puerto Rican draft-resisters hang out—some of those kids are legitimate hippies, running away from everything. You can't miss them on the road, because of their long hair and dirty clothes. We have a lot of short-haired 'hippies' in Puerto Rico, with good clothes, but those communes don't want them. 'Too many of that kind,' they say, 'and we don't need them.' The one in Orocovis, in the mountains, is a farm with a few shacks. Most of the boys and girls sleep outdoors in sleeping bags and carry their belongings in a blanket. They say they are there simply to *be.*

"In El Yunque [a famous rain forest], there is a religious commune, that was started by an ex-member of MPI. They say they are 'yippies' [the members of the Youth International Party]."

National Anthem

These are the original nineteenth-century words of the Puerto Rican national anthem:

La Borinqueña

Despierta, Borinqueño	Awaken, Borinqueño,
que han dado la señal.	For the signal has been given.
Despierta de ese sueño	Awaken from this sleep,
que es hora de luchar.	For it is the hour of struggle.
A ese llamar patriotico	If that patriotic call
no arde tu corazón.	Does not ignite your heart,
Ven te será simpatico	Come! You will respond
el ruido del cañon.	To the sound of the cannon.
Nosotros queremos la libertad	We want Liberty—
Nuestro machete nos la dará.	Our machete will give it to us!
Vámonos, Borinqueño	Let's go, Borinqueño.
Vámonos ya,	Let's go now,
que nos espera ansiosa	For she awaits us eagerly,
ansiosa la libertad,	Eagerly—Liberty!
la libertad, la libertad,	Liberty—Liberty!
la libertad, la libertad.	Liberty—Liberty!

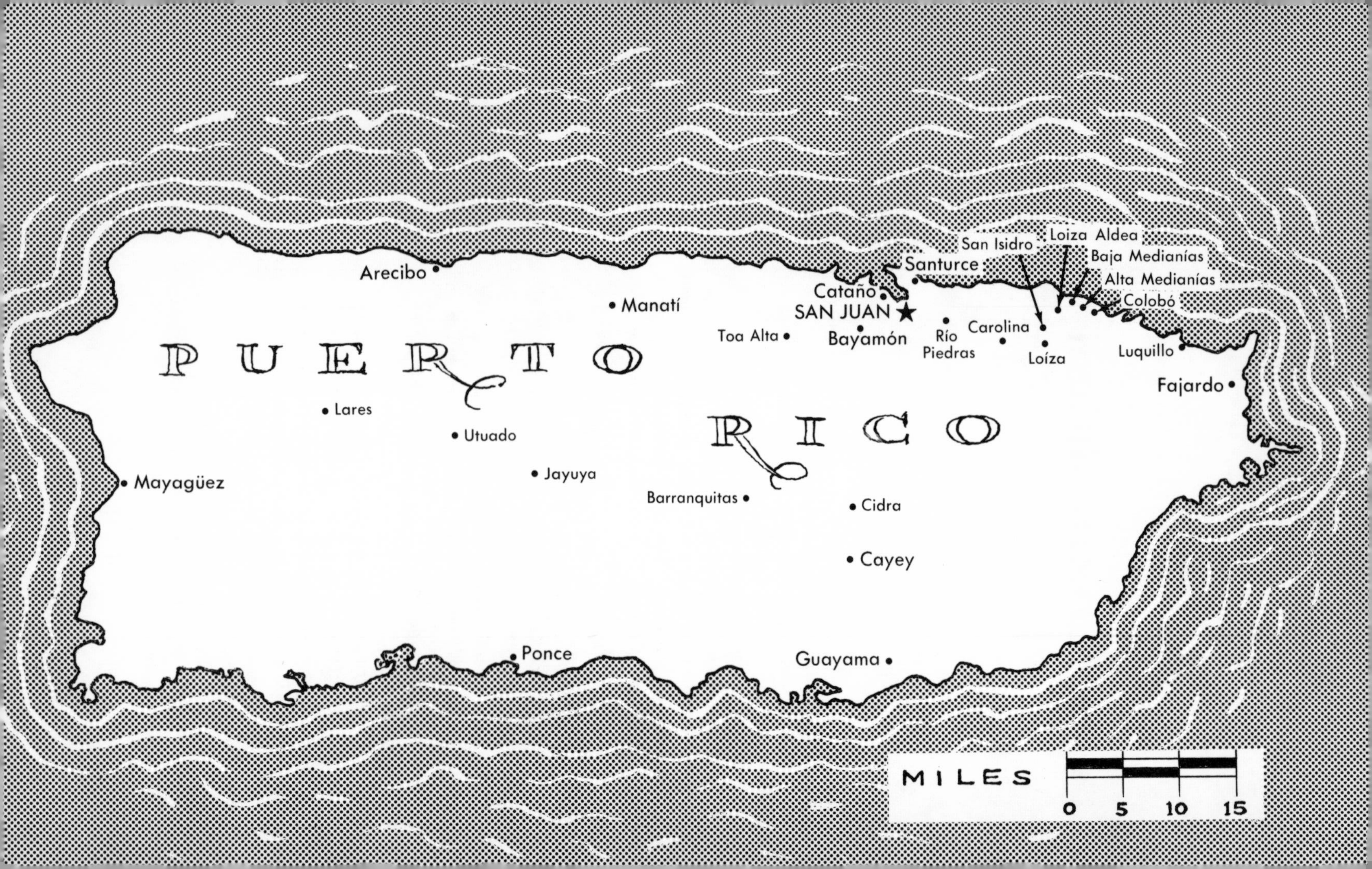
PUERTO RICO
Arecibo
Manatí
Santurce
San Isidro
Loiza Aldea
Baja Medianías
Alta Medianías
Colobó
Cataño
SAN JUAN
Toa Alta
Bayamón
Río Piedras
Carolina
Loíza
Luquillo
Fajardo
Lares
Utuado
Jayuya
Mayagüez
Barranquitas
Cidra
Cayey
Ponce
Guayama
MILES
0
5
10
15

Dates in Puerto Rican History

1493 November 19. Christopher Columbus discovers the Island and names it San Juan Bautista (Saint John the Baptist). Spaniards defeat the Tainos Indians.

1508 Colonial settlement begins at Caparra under governorship of Juan Ponce de León.

1509 First African slaves are brought to the island.

1511 Caparra's name is changed to Puerto Rico.

1521 The Island's name is changed to Puerto Rico. The capital is relocated and named San Juan. A period of expansion begins, marked by conflict with Carib Indians.

1533 La Fortaleza is built. San Juan becomes a strategic Caribbean defense center of the Spanish Empire but declines as a commercial port, with a ban on foreign shipping. Soon French, English, Dutch, and Danish privateers begin raids, which go on for more than two centuries.

1586 Mexico is required to pay an annual contribution to maintain San Juan's military establishment. Construction of El Morro fort is begun.

1595 The first assault on El Morro and San Cristóbal, led by Sir Francis Drake, is defeated.

1664 Governor Perez frees fugitive slaves from foreign colonies if they accept Catholicism and allegiance to Spain.

1700 Beginning of a century of smuggling in defiance of Spanish authorities.

1750 Coffee cultivation is begun.

1765 First census of the Island is taken: 44,883 inhabitants—39,846 free men, 5,037 slaves.

1797 Sir Ralph Abercromby leads last privateer assault and is defeated.

1809 Ramón Power y Giralt, a native Puerto Rican, is chosen as the Island's first representative to the Spanish *Cortes* (Parliament). In 1810, he is elected vice-president of the *Cortes*.

1815 August 10. Puerto Rico is opened to immigration, and free foreign trade is permitted.
Smuggling declines.

1868 Armed uprising for Independence occurs in Lares.

1880 In a reign of terror under General don Romualdo Palacios, many are imprisoned or exiled.

1897 Luis Muñoz Rivera wins Charter of Autonomy from Spain.

1898 July 25. In Spanish-American War, U.S. armed forces land at Guánica.
December 10. Treaty of Paris is signed: Puerto Rico is placed under U.S. sovereignty.

1900 First civilian government instituted under U.S. rule.

1916 Luis Muñoz Rivera, Puerto Rico's great liberator, dies.

1917 U.S. Congress passes Jones Act, providing U.S. citizenship for Puerto Ricans.

1942 Operation Bootstrap, an industrialization program, begins and continues through the 1950's.

1947 Jones Act is amended to allow Puerto Ricans to elect their own governor.

1949 January 2. Luis Muñoz Marín, son of Luis Muñoz Rivera and founder of Popular Democratic Party, takes office as first elected governor.

1950 July 3. Public Law 600: "The people of Puerto Rico may organize a government pursuant to a constitution of their own adoption."
October 30. Armed insurrection at Jayuya by nationalists is defeated. Pedro Albizu Campos and others are imprisoned.

1951 August. Ninety-two delegates are elected to a constitutional convention.

1952 July 25. Commonwealth of Puerto Rico is officially proclaimed; Spanish name—*Estado Libre Asociado.*

1967 July 23. In a plebiscite, Puerto Ricans vote to continue commonwealth form of government in association with United States.